I Confess
Revised Addition
Of Confessions Of
The Accused

Derrel Moore

Copyright © 2018 Derrel Moore

All rights reserved.

ISBN:1719489289
ISBN-9781719489287

DEDICATION

I dedicate this book to my daughter, De'aira, and her two little girls. I Pray through my story you'll find your own, and it will inspire you to be the best you. Your father loves you, please forgive me. I left me, long before I left you.

....

My sincere thanks to GOD, it is you alone that I Praise and you alone that I owe for my existence. Thank you for all of it, (Thank You).

To all those that helped me in life regardless of individual motives or the outcomes of those relationships, I thank God for having inspired you and I thank each of you for those efforts. I know I'm not the easiest to love or except help, but somehow you helped me and loved me anyway, Thank you, Thank you, THANK YOU.

Angie, I highlight you because you've been everything I needed exactly when I needed it, a true friend you remained regardless of the noise, thanks my Rose.

Nicole, you made me a father, I'll forever be grateful for that alone, but since then you've become a friend and I cherish that just as much.

To my Austin, and Moore families, as well as the extensions to each, I will forever be grateful to those who loved me through my process despite my failures.

Dina, you've been a friend when a friend is needed most, thanks and shout out to the ATL.

Since the writing of the original copy of this book there's been a few major events, some sad, one of which was the untimely death of my brother and friend, Shamel Parker, may your soul rest my brother, I love you. Ma Duke, and Grannie, thanks for showing me love, family forever.

Nickie you helped me grow, thanks for the love, the laughs and the knocks, I will never forget.

Jennifer, if not for you is all I need to say, thank you lady. Jassy God sent you for a reason and a season, thanks for being his servant and for having been a friend. I cherish it and regret the short comings.

So many have come in my life for a second or a minute to help me through a moment in time while I was in that dark place. You know who you are and you can trust I'll never forget, thank you, it helped in ways you'll never truly know.

Dad I can only imagine the pains you've experienced because of the decisions I've made in my life. Thanks for never giving up and for always loving me even as I made mistakes, struggling to get it right, you never failed to let me know you love me. Thanks Pops.

Granny Love and my grandfather may you both find peace and rest in it. The two of you showed me what real love looks like. My dearest Granny Love I'm going to do my best to pay all my debts in this life that I owe so one day we can meet again. I love you my lady.

Mom it would take a book to list my thanks, so I'm writing it. You were but a girl when you found out you were pregnant with me. With all your dreams of becoming a pop star ahead of you, and very possible, you chose me instead. You loved me like no other, your love for me was so selfish you refused to have more children, always telling me all your love was for me and you had no more left to give. I love how you did your best with the tools you possessed to raise me. Please know that it was because of you, "by God's permission", that I survived, and eventually figured out my reason why. I love you Doll.

A special thanks to my youngest most dedicated reader, and promoter, Willow Pillow. A special thanks to my uncles Robert, Ricky, and Mike, I learned valuable lessons from all of you. My cousin Ebony aka Pretty eyes, you know I love you, your more than just a cousin, your like my big sister, love you girl. May I love you like cook food. Chantilly

I Confess

please know I love you and I root for you in life. Aunt Wanda your my girl, I miss you and love you, you taught me the game, no one can beat me in spades, not even you, the master, lol.

Monique, Shawn, Nicole, Snapper, Nakia, Gina, Family matters, I forgive all of you and love you more than you know. Monet, know that I understand.

To all those I caused harm, please forgive me, now that I know better I promise I'll do better. As for those who hurt me in any…. way I forgive you and thank you for the lessons of growth. I learned from you.

CONTENTS

CHAPTER ONE: LESSONS CHILDREN SHOULDN'T LEARN

CHAPTER TWO: SEX EDUCATION AT SIX

CHAPTER THREE: SUFFERING LOSSES

CHAPTER FOUR: MY FIRST LOVE AFFAIR

CHAPTER FIVE: MY COMING OUT PARTY

CHAPTER SIX: TRUE TO HER WORD

CHAPTER SEVEN: NOW THEY FEAR ME

CHAPTER EIGHT: ONE MORE CHANCE

CHAPTER NINE: FRIENDS WITH A KILLER

CHAPTER TEN: RUNNING OUT OF TIME

CHAPTER ELEVEN: YOU CAN RUN BUT YOU CAN'T HIDE

CHAPTER TWELVE: THE TRUTH SHALL SET YOU FREE

CHAPTER THIRTEEN: WELCOMEBACK TO BUFFALO

CHAPTER FOURTEEN: A KID IN THE BIG HOUSE

CHAPTER FIFTEEN: SHE PROMISED SHE'D ALWAYS BE THERE

CHAPTER SIXTEEN: DEVASTATION INSPIRES CHANGE

CHAPTER SEVENTEEN: THANK GOD I SURVIVED BEING LIL DEE

Derrel Moore

INTRODUCTION

After many... years of warring with myself on the direction of this book, trying to choose the direction to take that will best serve, not just the youth chasing down my fate and forcing on my old shoes, but to provide the parents, elders and judicial system with a meaningful glimpse into the reality of the black boy lost.

He is no different than the suicide bomber who's desperate to draw attention to the plight of his people, willing to die in a irrational insane fashion, not in hopes of heaven but in hopes that someone will say; let me see what condition would cause this person to choose such a hopeless and dead end path, and most of all what can be done to address that condition so no one else will ever feel that hopeless, and purposely claim that wrath.

Well I'm one of the hopeless, I've answered our cry/call, because so... far no one else has, at least with the answer we can relate to! so as I sit here captivated in a far corner of the world my only escape into abyss of the norm.

This is my truth, at first I planned to write it in a novel like form, change names, and places, but that would only allow the lies to live, and the truth would be lost in the glory of the madness of the mad. I can't lay here, and wallow in the misery waiting on more company. I have more than I can stomach, this is a cry, no a ROAR, use it to understand us that are lost, then if you dare to judge, dare to save, because God created us, we're worth saving, we're more valuable than you know.

Personally *I had to lose everything before I found the strength to save myself, but still I sit captivated, so... much to offer, but all I have is prison bars, and toilets to clean. If you dare to judge, dare to save!!!*

To my fallen peers, I pray they'll get the message but for you are strong enough read my story feel and feed of my pain, then save yourself because for most of us just like the suicide bomber there's no savior there's no understanding they'll lie in wait to judge/kill you. So if you can, I beg you, don't live my life, learn it, and then run from it! Trust me it's full of death; hate, loss and regret.

To those I hurt, I don't offer my excuses, it is so... true that hurt people, hurt people, but this book is no excuse for my behavior I take responsibility for my actions and I apologize for them. I pray that anyone I've ever hurt or ever caused any pain can one day find peace and forgive me for my ignorant behavior. Unfortunately, as well as fortunately we live as we learn and as I've grown to know better I've done better. I can't take back my yesterdays or the mistakes I've made in them, but I can do better today now that I know better.

All I can hope for is that the world over will take a look at my experience in the inner city of what we label as "the ghetto", and better understanding the black boy. We are crying for help as we rush to trade in our school books for drugs, guns and prison cells. We want the American dream as much as anyone, but we are born into a nightmare and as the resilient adaptable human beings that we are we adjusted to this reality pretty quickly. We became masters of it, as we took the word nigger and turned it into a sociable word of endearment we took hunting and killing each other as a sport making it just as common!

This is no coincidence we feel worthless so we act worthless. We were born into this we didn't ask for this hate we inherited this evil. Sadly we've somehow been able to (con)vince the world over that there's no hope for us and the world over has decided to take this con to heart leaving us to destroy each other out of emotions we don't quite understand at fourteen and fifteen years old.

I ask that you not discard us. I ask that before you judge us get to know us and then if you dare to judge dare to save. I ask that you roll up your sleeves get your hands dirty help to save the next out of control child you see boy or girl. Don't be the person that has an opinion but no solution. Don't be the one that sits high and look low, but don't know.

This book is not just my story it's our story and it's our problem. We can pretend it don't exist if we're foolish enough. We can continue to watch kids like me go to prison with life sentences for crimes they can't even "spell" let alone understand the consequence of, or we can learn some of the problems are and do something about them.

The truth will hurt some feelings some of my families secrets will be exposed and it's not pretty. My father will feel betrayed and as I reveal this raw truth it is very humbling because some of my facades must be destroyed. My entire family will never look at me the same. My daughter will know this she never knew. this is not easy and it is very scary but it is necessary. I can't know better and ignore my obligation to do better.

So here it is read my truth. Just remember if you dare to judge dare to save...

Derrel Moore

Confessions Of The Accused

1 CHAPTER

LESSONS CHILDREN SHOULDN'T LEARN

At five years old I had the best a child could have; two loving parents together and in love. I was in school and had lots of friends. I remember wanting to be a fireman when I grew up. I wanted to be a hero save people from burning homes, and buildings no one could tell me I wouldn't grow up to be a hero just like superman. Wow I've come so... far.

My mother, whose real name is Sylvia Darlene Austin. Was the well-built beautiful black woman. She had curves that men die for; her skin caramel brown, she was no more than five foot even, gorgeous almond shaped brown eyes, and a voice that reminds you of Whitney Houston. Just a few short verses and you'd want her to sing all day. She would tell me she chose me over her own dreams of becoming a superstar and I'm not alone when I tell you she could have made it.

My father whose real name is Derrel Lemorne Moore Sr; was her exact opposite, where she was short, and petite with curves, he was tall and huge. A man's man the kind woman fall for at first sight. He had the brightest smile and could charm a woman in sixty seconds flat a trait that often got him in trouble. Tall dark and handsome with the devils tongue to match but there was no doubt he loved my mother. They were childhood sweethearts and the world was theirs to conquer.

Then one summer day as I dreamed the innocent naïve dreams that five year old boys have I was awakened by the screams of my mother. I was confused I didn't know what was going on but I knew my mom was being hurt and I was on course to growing up to be a hero. So I ran to her screams with sleep in my eyes void of fear in my heart. I was going to protect my mother at all cost after all I was a hero and I wanted to be hers.

When I burst into the door of the bedroom I saw a sight I've never been able to shake my mother was laying on the bed crying out in pain and instead of some monster or strange man it was my own father. he was beating my mother the look on her face to see her own son witness such madness from the man responsible for showing me how to be a man hurt her to the core. The look in his eyes as he told me to get out cut me bone deep. If I had to guess I'd say in that instant I started to change.

My fantasy of life was about took a blow it was never to recover from. I loved my parents but in that instant my little confused heart was forced to choose and on my mother's face was pain; love, and regret, all for me being forced to see her this way! On my father's face was rage; anger, and denial, traits I later became intimate with, but traits it took me long time to know where I learned them from.

I rejected the demands of my father to get out "the first time I had openly defied him" and the hero in me jumped on his back all thirty odd pounds of me screaming, kicking and punching him. Get off my mommy I screamed but he was far too gone, he raised up from the position where he was bent over my mother beating her and I was forced to stop hitting him, and hang on. He's a pretty big guy well over six feet. For a five year old he looked like a giant! He tossed me off his back the fall was long, scary, and felt very violent. He started in on my mother again but seen that I was getting up and I don't know what came over him, but he left the house in rage.

....

After we were done crying consoling each other and mourning `our respective loss, my mom got me dressed as well as herself and we walked hand and hand down Jefferson Avenue in Buffalo, New York to Landon street and to a place we always found as sanctuary when times got tough "granny's house". A home where even a stranger could go to find peace one could find refuge and a good meal.

It was here where wounds got licked and hearts got healed. It is the love I got and learned from my grandparents in which I cling on to now. This love and example of theirs is what I call on in recent times to find my way back from a life of pain. I call on that love in order to open up to tell my truth.

When we finally made it to my grandparent's house we came in all smiles and some story my mom made up and made me go along with in order to keep things calm. We would learn latter that my granny love "my mother's mom" was no fool she knew something was wrong. She always knew but her house was where you could run to for love not where you'd be judged.

My grandmother, Sylvia Beatrice Austin, was just as small in stature as my mom she was just the heavy set version. She had the heart of a lioness, she'd fight for all that she loved, and my grandmother loved everyone. Although my grandmother and mother looked alike besides their weight my grandmother despite her knocks in life had this peace about her that was admirable. She had so... many past experiences that she could have used as an excuse to be bitter but her faith in God allowed her to not let life knock her down without her getting right back up.

My grandfather, James 'Bootsie' Drakeford, who was not my mother's biological father was truly my only real example growing up of what a man is. He met my grandmother after she had several bad experiences with men. At the time she met my grandfather she had four children by different men. At the time my mother was a toddler and my uncle mike was a newborn but my grandfather treated her as the beautiful queen that she was. This was the nineteen sixties, a time when an unwed mother was outcast but he treated her as a queen.

My grandfather was dark as night in complexion; average in height, about five foot eight inches tall, with the character of a giant. He loved my grandmother's four children and the baby girl they had together all the same they were a family, nowhere near perfect but a family indeed.

As this day started with violence and confusion went on my mother did the best she could to make me forget the traumatizing event that we had experienced. We didn't talk about it at all we pretended it didn't happen. She fed me my favorite foods and I was allowed to go outside to play with my friends. Most of my friends lived right there on Landon street. For me this was home it was on Landon street where my heart was. I ran up, and down, and played until night stole the day. By this time the beauty of the mind of a child one of God's gifts allowed me to forget the earlier trouble and was able to just be a kid.

Bootie!!! Bootie!!! It was my mother she had the most beautiful voice I've ever heard to this day but she also had the loudest voice I've ever heard and when she was looking for me let's just say the entire neighborhood knew about it. Bootie was her pet name for me and it got me teased a lot by my friends everyone knows kids can be cruel without even realizing it, and my friends where no different. That cost me and I always had to fight for my respect.

After the very infamous screams of Bootie from my mother I came in the house got washed up and ate my favorite foods. Back then I could eat macaroni and cheese with pork chops every day. there was no one that could make that macaroni and cheese like my mom. don't get me wrong my Granny love was the best cook ever but my mother's macaroni wow! After eating my favorite foods I was too tired to even realize I was no longer at my mom and dad's house in my own bed that was huge and fit for a prince. Instead I was at my Granny's house in my heart of hearts this was home.

Again I was sleeping like a baby dreaming again only to once again wake up to violent noise. This time it was many voices as well as violent sounds. I heard the voice of my mom; my dad, my uncle, my grandparents and aunt Wanda. The hero in me was once again awakened. I ran to my mother's aid as I saw my mother, grandparents, and aunt trying to pull at my uncle. He was fighting with my father, violently hitting him telling him to keep his hands off his sister. My mother was crying begging him to stop saying she loves my father and to please leave him alone. My uncle Robert looked at her like she was crazy then left in what can only be described as rage, and disgust.

My mother turned to try to console my father but he acted as if she'd broken their bond and trust. He left the house upset as if he was the one who had been her victim earlier that morning. My mother cried and I did my best to console her as she held me tight. It was hard I was five years old, my life was perfect yesterday but now I was afraid that every time I went to sleep something bad would happen! As I write this true I now realize why to this very day many… moons later I still struggle with sleep. I fight it off, and then when I need I'm forced to fight for it, up but no matter what sleep has been my enemy since that summer when I turned five years old.

………………………………………………..

After a few days my mom and dad made up. They never asked for my opinion after all I was just a kid and in truth at the time I most likely wouldn't have the ability to express myself. I was scared my father had become a monster to me. Where it was easy to talk to him I was now reserved. I had to watch what I said and mostly I said nothing. My mother only needed a few days maybe dinner and make up sex. I don't know, but I know I needed him to give me back the security and safety he'd stolen from me. Instead I got a dog and still to this day we never had that talk which explains why our bond although there is still strained.

My dad got me a dog and I fell instantly in love with him. He was all I had to talk to when I was at my mom and dad's house. My mother and father were in love and young love knows no bounds. They loved me but they really didn't know or understand what I needed. I would talk to my dog tell him everything I was afraid to say to them. I was scared. I didn't look at my father the same and I couldn't sleep. I barely ate. I was confused and lived in fear that my dad would hurt us again. I say us because you don't get to hurt a child's mother without simultaneously hurting that child.

My parents kept asking me to name my dog, but I couldn't even think of one. I was in a state of depression at the age of five years old. My mom would ask me what was wrong, my favorite word was nothing but inside of me it screamed (everything!). I would beg to go home. My mom would say you are at home. So I'd say I want to go to my Granny house! My mom tried to break me out of it but my home was where my heart was and that was 85 Landon street.

………………………………………………………….

I'll never forget this day it was close to school time. I was kind of nervous but I was also excited. All my friends were at school #53. I couldn't wait to see them because I didn't get to see them much only when I was at my Granny house. After the fight with my uncle and my dad my father didn't want us over there much. However on this day he dropped us off he had things to do. So I went to see my "Granny love" that's what I called her. I gave the biggest hug and immediately I was out of my shell. I don't know if my mom noticed but I would blossom when my father wasn't around.

I went outside to play with my friends. I told them about my cool new dog and promised I'd bring him the next time. I still hadn't given him a name so my friends and I started thinking of names. I was thinking of Dino just like Fred Flintstone pet. I had a lot of fun that day. Then I heard my mom calling with that infamous nickname she gave me Bootie. I would try to ignore her I couldn't stand that name but my friends would tell me your mother calling you Bootie! I would end up rolling in the dirt with one of them play fighting because they called me Bootie. I just didn't like anyone but her to use it. My aunt Wanda would call me that even my mom's friend Yolanda. There was a select few that would call me that but as I got older I would only answer to one person calling me that. I think my mother who lasted the longest calling me that. She told me that she called me that because after she had me she got a bootie (smile).

I finally stop rolling in the dirt in back of 77 Landon street with my friends over them getting on me about my name. my mother's voice was getting louder and closer so I tried to dust myself off as I ran out the front to answer her, smile on my face trying to hide the mischievous behavior. When I got out there I noticed my father's car a red and white boxer. My smile vanished as I realized he was back and we were leaving. I begged to stay to no avail. I went back to the house to say my goodbyes to Granny love. My grandfather who I called "Bootsie" like everyone else was at work he worked all day and night to take care of his family.

After saying my goodbyes I reluctantly approached the car with my mother and father inside. I got in the backseat my father greeted me, I returned his greeting, but it was obvious to everyone in the car it wasn't very exciting. He pulled off down Landon I waved to my friends knowing I probably wouldn't see them again until school started although I only lived around the corner on Jefferson avenue. When we pulled in the driveway I was looking forward to being able to see my dog. I finally had a name in mind for him it had been a couple of weeks it was time to give him a name.

I didn't see him on his chair in the backyard. I was looking for him he was just a puppy because he wasn't house broken yet my dad put him outside when we left. I looked and looked but couldn't find my dog. My dad looked around, nothing and then he took me inside. I was crying about my dog my mother was scared of all animals but she felt my pain and asked my dad to find my dog. My dad went back out to talk to the neighbors when he returned some time later he had the dog leash and a sad look on his face. He didn't know how to tell me what happened to my dog so he told my mom. The neighbor's dog had got loose he got in our yard and killed my dog. I was devastated I didn't understand why another dog would do this. I cried like a baby and it was here in that moment that I learned it's a dog eat dog world.

A few days later after a lot of crying my dad came in with a pair of jeans. He told me they were from the neighbor. His dog ate my dog and he sent me a pair of jeans! My grief turned to anger it's my first memory of rage but I held it in. I couldn't trust my father with my feelings. He had become an object to fear. There was no doubt he loved me but I just couldn't forget that look in his eyes when he was attacking my mother.

....

By this time school was in session and I went with a chip on my shoulder. I was five years old but I was a wise five. I went to school knowing that fathers beat mothers; dogs eat dogs, and I was afraid to sleep because bad things happen whenever I do. I would lay in bed at night my bed was right next to my parent's it was a big bedroom in a one bed room apartment. My mom and dad didn't know I was having trouble sleeping. So they would wait to come to bed thinking I was asleep. They'd smoke their weed in the living room; listen to music, then come to bed long after I should be asleep, and they'd have sex.

I went to school at five years old exposed to so... many of life's realities. My fantasies no longer existed. I still held on to my dream of being a fireman but my perfect life was over. I was a kid with issues, with a chip on my shoulders. I had no one to talk to; my dog was dead, and school #53 there was no outlet for troubled kids. All troubled kids got back then was sent to the principal's office where we'd be threatened to get a trip to see Mr. Patterson. A teacher known to use his paddle on the behinds of kids that misbehaved.

   I was defiant. I had no fear of Mr. Patterson or his paddle. I carried on, did just enough in school to be deemed smart. I never really acted out too much that year I had no real obvious problems. I was more of an introvert that year. Most of my problems that year were in my head; heart, and at home.

   There were more fights with my mother and father but they learned to keep them under wraps so it wouldn't involve me. At least that's what they told themselves. They argued a lot my mom accused my father of cheating all the time. We would move in and out. It would be good for a week bad for a week. It went back and forth. I became insecure and grew distant from my father even more. I would see my mother cry over and over. I couldn't help her. I felt helpless and I blamed him. In all of their fighting, and all the noise. I was the casualty but they had no way of knowing just what their behavior was doing to me.

   Then I remember my grandmother my father's mother passed away and it was the worst thing to happen to us. We were already a very fragile and dysfunctional family and losing her destroyed us. My father loved this woman beyond all measure and so did I. she was just this great woman full of nothing but love. Then she was gone. All I remember is her love she truly loved me and would never allow my father to be less than a man to me. So when she passed a part of me did as well.

   I remember the day of her funeral. I jumped on her casket as the pawl barriers took her casket from the church and begged to go with her. I don't remember much else but her love and that I wanted to go too. Something in me knew things would change, and they did.

Derrel Moore

Derrel Moore
Confessions Of The Accused

CHAPTER TWO

SEX EDUCATION AT SIX

After a while my mother couldn't deal with my father anymore and she told me we were moving out for good. We were back at my grandparent's house and I was in heaven. I was doing well in school. My mother was out on the town. On the days she wasn't chasing after my father, she was out with her girls clubbing. She was so... young. She was pregnant with me at the age of seventeen my father was all she knew. She hadn't really lived. So she would go out and my Granny Love would get sick of it. She'd load me up in her car and go from bar to bar looking for her. I remember one night my Granny Love found her at this bar called the 133. She went in dragged her out; told her she's a mother, got a son to raise, so she don't get to roam the streets all night every night! My Granny Love gave her an ear full, then put her in the car to take her home. As we drove up the street my mother jumped out of the moving car. She rolled in the street then jumped up running away. My mom was drunk and high, but most of all she was hurt. I looked just like my daddy and she couldn't bear it. She was running from so much more than I could understand back then but for me it seemed like she was running from me.

This kind of behavior went on for a while but Granny Love took care of me. She would do her best to guide her child (my mother) out of the darkness but she would never miss a beat when it came to loving me. Then out of nowhere my mom forgave my father and with no warning we were moving back in with him.

This time it was on the other side of town. He moved on Delaware Ave. this was downtown Buffalo, N.Y. in a prominently white neighborhood. I was far from my friends, and more distant than ever from my father. I hadn't really seen him much. It was like when they broke up and it only made the strain on our father/son relationship worse.

Men, I implore you don't allow the relationship or lack of a relationship with the mother of your child or child to be what determines the kind of relationship you have with your kid(s). there's simply no excuse that will do and they will never understand.

By this time my father was openly dealing drugs. I never knew him to work at this time or prior. I never knew or thought to question his income but by this time I was growing rapidly. I was being exposed to all kinds of things. So there was no shock on my behalf to move back in with my father and learn he was dealing weed. Even if he wanted to he couldn't hide it. We lived in a studio apartment and he literally had a garbage bag twice my size full of weed sitting in the bedroom area of the apartment. I use to play on it like it was a bean bag.

They would party and deal drugs right there. I think they lied to themselves. In their heads I was too young to understand. I sure wouldn't be able to remember it later in life or be able to comprehend it all. These are the lies people tell themselves in order to carry on in such a reckless manner. The reality is if a child can see or hear that child can retain what he or she sees or hears. I stand as a living testament to having both heard and having seen way too much. For all you parents that are blessed to have little gifts born to you by the direct permission of God, be careful what you show that gift and what you allow that gift to hear.

By the time I turned six years old I was struggling with my issues with my father. Things were a little better but I still didn't trust him. There was always confusion with him and my mother over him cheating on her. This would cause her to pick up and leave with me being dragged along for the ride. We could be gone a day or month it all depended on how long it would take for them to work it out. There was one thing that was for sure, my dad didn't know how to be a father when they broke up, and my mother really didn't know how to let him be one.

Whenever they weren't together and he would try and see me there was always serious drama. I remember him coming to get me to take me places and it would start out being about me, but it always ended up all about them. This put that much more distance between my father and I. It isolated me and made it easy for me to fall victim in this world of sickness where hurt people, hurt people.

I was six years old and I had so many emotions inside me that I couldn't articulate back then. My mother had found out my father was out cheating and we once again moved back to my grandparent's house. I was happy because I was tired of the fights and at least here I could relax. I was always on edge when I was home alone with my parents. It was very tense for me. So being back at my grandparent's house I was free to be a kid whenever I was at the house of love that was void of confusion. At this house I knew what to expect and that was stability.

This time around was much different. This trip was unlike any other I can remember. I had a very traumatic experience that likely caused me to go on an out of control roller coaster ride to make a effort to take control of my sexuality. I have never been able to shake this experience and I'm fighting to find the words to express it. However I must because it's the lie that has been allowed to live which has caused so much pain. It's the lie that allowed me to indifferently hurt others and myself for so long. It must never do so again.

One day I was playing with all my friends, my cousins and their friends. We ranged in ages from as young as me at the time, to teenagers. It was a fun day, I was having the time of my little young life. The mind of a child is so innocent, and we know no evil in our hearts so we can't see it coming. A older cousin of mines use to tickle me until I'd almost cry. I hated it but loved the chase and the attention. All day he was playing with everyone and we had a great time. We were all on landon street, down the street from my grandparent's house at my great grandmothers house, Grandma Pearl. She was this four foot ten inch unsung hero. The kind of person they don't make no more. She will forever be the one that got away from us all. My cousin Tim, "the tickler", lived with her. Tim was the light skinned out of shape big kid. He was more of a loner for the most part, not many friends, he had bad breath, body odor and man boobs. People would pick on him a lot and avoid him when it came to most gatherings. He was grown, about nineteen at the time but his only interaction was with the kids really.

After a while I got thirsty and wanted something to drink. So I went inside Grandma Pearl house. she wasn't home and all the kids were taking full advantage. Playing on the pouch and in the backyard. After i got some good old lemonade the kind that was always in the refrigerator back in the days with real lemons and ice. I was headed back out to play but got caught by my cousin Tim. He told me to come here. He was in the doorway of his bedroom which was right before you go back out of the house. He said I want to show you something I was a little nervous because I thought he was going to tickle me but he promised he wouldn't went inside his room.

When we got inside his room he shut the door, and I thought he tricked me but he told me to calm down. He just wanted to show me something, but I couldn't tell nobody. I thought he was going to show me some kind of secret treasure or something. I didn't but he had me curious so I was just willing to be quiet and let him show me. He said look if I wanted to tickle you I could as he put his hand gently on my stomach. I was nervous but he made me relax as he softly touched my stomach to build my trust. I said okay and he told me to just relax. He was going to show me something. I said okay because I believed he wasn't tricking me, and I trusted him. He told me to close my eyes first so I did then he chose to take my trust and destroy it.

He tugged at my shorts and before I knew it he was undoing my shorts, and my superman underwear was down and I was scared again. I opened my eyes and tried to pull away. I started to fight but he held me tight and covered my mouth. He told me to calm down he said didn't I tell you I wasn't going to tickle you? I just want to show you something calm down. I was nervous and scared but quiet. By this time I was going back into my shell. My cousin was big just like my father. I was scared beyond measure and I just stood still. He then bent over and put my innocent private parts into his mouth. I pulled back he lifted up and took his penis out. I was really scared now! He told me I should do the same thing to him. I pulled up my clothes struggled to hurry up and open the door. When I got it open I ran up the street to Granny Love house.

I was going to tell what he had done to me; but by the time I got there I felt guilty; I felt dirty, and I was ashamed. The more I thought about it I thought it was my fault and I didn't have no one to talk to. this has been my demon and burden alone since that very day.

I tried my best from that day to just avoid him touching me ever again. After that day I'd do my best to never be alone with him or allow him to catch me and tickle me. His hands were no longer hands I wanted anywhere near me! I couldn't get what he had done out of my head and my six year old mind became consumed with sexual thoughts. I was at odds with my sexuality. I questioned it and for many years I found myself trying to prove myself to myself. I never had any further incidents like this with this monster again but I couldn't get it out my head. Which caused me to act out in many ways.

....

A few weeks passed and I broke my entire right leg playing hero. I got in the middle of my mother play fighting with one of our female cousins. She was my mother's age name Ronnie. I learned to stay out the middle of women fights the hard way. After I got my first of many casts for this broken leg my mother allowed me to go to one of my favorite cousin's house for a few days.

I loved everything about being there. At the time my cousin stayed on Northumberland street. Being at my cousin May house was like a kid being at their favorite park 24-7. My cousin Mae had three kids. Monique was the oldest; Shawn was her middle child, and Ebony was the baby. She was also the closest in age to me. She had me by a few years. We always hung out she's one of my all-time favorite cousins.

The reason why I loved to go over May house is because she was a sweetheart. She'd give us anything she could. We could get away with murder at her house and she had a heart of gold. May is this big caramel skinned woman with big brown eyes. She could hardly read and wasn't the smartest woman but i dare you find one that loves harder than she does. All the kids loved staying at her house when we were young and I know to this day she still has a heart of gold.

I had a broken leg but I was still happy to be there and the leg wasn't going to slow me down. I was still having just as much fun as everyone else. I was doing so much running around; play fighting, and trying to ride a bike with one leg. That I had to go to the hospital a few times to get a new cast because I kept breaking them. My mother would be so... mad, but she felt a bit guilty that she broke my leg. Plus she could see the joy in me and she never knew how to tell me no much, or for too long.

I had a little girlfriend named Mickey. My older cousin Shawn was messing around with her sister and I had her. We were little kids but we looked up to them. Shawn was like my brother. I would do anything he told me to or that I saw him do back then. One night while May was out at bingo and none of the other adults of the house were home. We were tearing the house up having a good time. Then all the older kids started to disappear with their boyfriends or girlfriends. They went to rooms upstairs or left the house all together.

Mickey, who was almost a year older than me at the time lived a few doors down from my cousin's house. She was this light skinned pretty girl with long jet black hair. We went down to sit on her porch when all the older kids did their disappearing act. My cousin Shawn told us to go outside. We were to young for what was about to go down. We sat on her porch for a little while. Then we decided to sneak back into my cousin house to see what was going on. We quietly came in the house and right there in the living room we saw my cousin Shawn on top of Mickey's sister. They were having sex. I was a six year old expert by then. So I knew what they were doing. We watched them for a minute. Then I got an idea and took Mickey upstairs with me. We started to kiss and imitate what we saw downstairs.

   We took off all our clothes. I was only six but I felt older and it felt right. Plus I wanted and needed to get that image out of my head that my cousin Tim had put there by abusing me. As I think back on those times now I know that was the beginning of me trying to prove myself to myself. I would go on for years trying to prove my sexuality to myself and take back my power from that moment. Abuse is ugly; it hurts, and there is no predicting in what manner the person abused will deal with in pain. Mickey and I had our first sexual experience together the abuse didn't count. We fumbled around and after a number of seconds as well as a few pumps I had the urge to pee. I got up ran to the bathroom and it was over.

   I became extremely sexual for my age at that point. I was basically a little pervert. It wasn't cute at all. It was a sign of things to come but there was no one around that recognized the signs. I was exposed to so... much so... young, and there was no way my under developed child brain could handle all of it.

   The cerebrum which is the portion of the brain that contains our ability to reason and think intelligently had yet to develop. On the other hand my pituitary gland which affects all normal functions had been wrongfully stimulated. This caused me to act out sexually without reason; regard, or any intelligence.
   I was a child living on my God giving instincts and not much else. I had no mature way to process the moans of my mother in the next bed

over. Nor the mouth of a sick disgusting family member robbing me of a chance to live a life void of such a heavy burden. I had yet to develop an intellect. So I had no choice of doing anything close to intelligent. Truth be told my parents were just kids who had yet to fully develop in these ways. There was simply no chance I could properly deal with this at this time. Something that most victimizers are able to recognize when they pick their victims. I make no excuses. I chose a road that most don't but it can't be denied that I did so under extreme circumstances.

After my experience with Mickey I was open. In that moment I was free. I had no memory of the incident with the boogey man. He couldn't make me question why me in that moment so I needed more. I had to find ways to escape, and I found plenty. I had no boundaries. They had been stolen, and there was no way to know what was off limits. The only thing I knew was I had zero desire to see another man's penis. I started to experiment with other girls I was around all the time. I know this is a taboo subject, but this is my truth. In fat its a lot more than mines so I must not hold back.

As kids we are very curious, but be lack intellect. We're driven by intuition; observation of others and desires to be liked. As well as please the people we like/love. When this is combined with over exposure to behaviors that should be reserved for adults. Then you get children doing things they shouldn't. As well as leaving them vulnerable to be victimized by people like my cousin. This is dangerous, and parents should be mindful of what they expose their children to so they won't be harmed at the hands of others or their own hands.

I started to experiment with my girl cousins. I was a kid but I was doing things some adults still have yet to get around to doing. Or even have a desire to do. I can remember being in the room spending the night at Mae house again; it was me, and two of my girl cousins who were slightly older than me. We were all staying the night at Mae house as all the kids would back then. I won't say their names because my truth don't need to hurt them, or anyone for that matter. This is to help not harm and I don't know if they are ready to be as candid as me.

Those two cousins and I were supposed to be sleep. Instead we closed the door to the room, and we began to experiment all three of us. They were about nine at the time but we'd all been exposed to way too much. They asked me to kiss them on their private parts their vaginas. At first I said hell no but they talked me into it with the promises to never tell. After I did it to both of them they started picking on me. They started laughing saying my breath smelled like pootang. I was embarrassed and it would be a cold day in hell before a girl tricked me into doing that again!

This experiment started the three of us on our sexual relationship with each other. I basically had a threesome at six years old and I wasn't stopping there. I started to be with one of them every chance we got but not all three together again. I would always jump up running to the bathroom to pee after a few seconds of poking my little thing in one of them.

I could easily avoid this subject. I could do what most before me has, and make it pretty where in reality it was something altogether different. As bad as I'd like to pretend. I must stay the course so the truth of the man can be measured and not just isolated acts that have been highlighted as if that is all I am, or ever will be.

I had no business being exposed to the things I was at such a young age, but who would know this? My mother had me at a very young age. She was only eighteen years old when I was born. She barely knew much about life, and her own cerebrum was yet to fully develop. There was simply no way that a child was capable of raising a child without making come critical mistakes along the way. It would be easy to blame her, but she was never the root cause or the real reason nor was my father. The two of them did the best they could with the little they did knew. I have played the blame game in so... many of life's situations. It's easy to label someone; to judge them, and move on. What's had is understanding them then addressing their issues or your own.

I can go on with more of my incestuous stories or tell you how even when I went back to school that following year my mind was completely occupied with sex. I would flirt with girls ask to see this or feel that. I even learned who best to approach and who I shouldn't. I became a miniature victimizer. Learning how to spot easy targets that had low self-esteem. In being groomed by the sick minded man who had abused me. I learned how to do the same thing in a sense. At the age of six I had been sexually educated in the worse way.

Like I said, I can highlight more examples of what I'd been exposed to. As well as my own twisted learning behaviors. However I believe that the point on this subject is made. This was a critical time in my life it caused me to set out on a new course. I was no longer on a course to be a big hero saving children from burning fires. I was on fire deep down inside my soul. Running from my boogey man. Never realizing I had become my own worst enemy. I wouldn't learn this for many years and many people would become a casualty in the process of me finding my way back to my truth. My dream was to be a hero and I can only pray that many are saved from this truthful account.

Derrel Moore
Confessions Of The Accused

CHAPTER THREE

SUFFERING LOSSES

By the time I was eight years old my mother and father were finally done with the merry go round. She had moved out and did her best to try to move on they would still have their moments they loved each other but I think they were both done with trying to make it work. My father had stopped dealing. My mother had found him a job when we were still living on Delaware. She convinced this guy to give him a chance in his construction business. My father knew nothing about construction but my mom made him, try him out and he was a nitrile. He was good with his hands and a fast learner.

So he had a nice job by this time and was never around much. I would only see my father on special occasions; birthdays, holidays if a carnival was in town, or when I really messed up, and he would come and whip my butt. It was so traumatic for me not to see my father for two months and then out of nowhere he would show up to beat me for being bad. I'm not saying I wasn't bad or didn't deserve and very much need some discipline. It was just hard getting it from a stranger that I was afraid of. This was a man I seen hurt my mom in many different ways. Seen him physically beat her and emotionally destroy her. I had no connection to him really even on days he'd come with a smile bearing gifts. I didn't know how to except his efforts.

The thing is "I needed him" and deep down I loved him more than I knew how to express. I would practice what I'd say the next time I'd see him (I still do this) but back then when I would see him I could never get the words out. I could practice for hours and I could count the words on one hand that I spoke to him. I wanted to tell this man (my older cousin that hurt me) had hurt me; I wanted to tell him that I missed him and needed to see him more. I had questions that only a man can answer but I needed him around first. He had stolen my security at five. I still hadn't recovered in fact I'd become worse. I really needed him but my little heart instinctively knew he wasn't capable of being the man I need him to be.

I would here my mother rant and rave about him. she would call him every name in the book. Which didn't make my own view of him any better. I was 100% dependent on her. She was the constant of the two in my life. I would listen to her and her words one by one destroyed him as a man. His behaviors wouldn't make it any better. If anything they gave her words more power but it didn't make the words right on her action correct.

What my mother failed to consider is that I didn't just look like my dad I was part of him and she conveniently forgot all the good qualities that made her love him. She allowed her pain to rip him apart. She simultaneously ripped me apart as well. I'm sure she didn't mean to but the more she talked badly about him the more insecure I became. After all I looked like this man and came from his loins.

This became the norm. time passed and I would see my father less. My mother became bitter as he moved on with ease. She felt like they belonged together. She felt like she made him who he was slowly becoming. I remember how'd she run her list down; I helped that bastard with school work, he could barely read and wright, if it wasn't for me he would have never graduated. I gave him a son. I dropped my education to take care of our family. I got that fool that job. I begged to get him that job he'd still be doing nothing if it wasn't for me! The list would go on and it would confuse me as to who my father was. I really had my own issues with him to sort out but her words just didn't make me question him in my head they made me question who I was and who I'd become.

The one thing I knew for sure from her words is that I didn't want to be anything like him. I was a momma's boy. I loved her more than life so I didn't want to be like the man she seemed to hate. What she failed to consider was how confused that left me. I didn't have many good examples; my uncles where either in prison, on drugs, or selling drugs by this time. The one constant was my grandfather he was a hardworking man always there for us. He was exactly what I now aspire to be. But at a such young age I really couldn't see past the shortcomings of the man I looked like.

Again I didn't blame my mother she was a child with a child. At twenty-six years old she was hardly prepared to deal with the complex issues I already had. In fact she couldn't even recognize them. I was just another wild out of control kid growing up in the "hood". I wasn't the only one and my behavior didn't raise any red flags. All it raised was more belts more often to whoop my butt. The more my mother would discredit my father the more I become confused and insecure. I would act out and she'd whoop my butt then call my father to do the same.

At this critical stage in my young life despite the traumatic experiences I'd had up to that point I still had a chance. After all I was just a kid with the right nurturing from my parents my young mind could have been repaired. The truth is my young parents who had me way too young lacked the tools necessary to properly nurture me. This is why it's so important for children that are coming into their young adulthood to not confuse this with being ready for a child of their own.

My mother turned my father into a weapon against me. He'd became the threat she'd use to get me to act right. Never realizing the conflict this left me in. I loved my father; I needed my father, I even missed him. But at the same time his actions and her words had caused me to fear him and somewhat dislike him. I don't think she ever stopped to realize that I wasn't just "her" child they were both blessed to have me together. They were both equally responsible for my nurturing. Somehow this was lost on her. She tried her best to be my mother and father but she failed miserably. A lie can never replace the truth no matter how well intended it may be. He was my father and both of them had a duty to see that he acted like one.

The only thing she successfully accomplished was helping to confuse me about who I was and ultimately this made me insecure. My father wasn't the best role model but he was the most important for a child my age. I needed my father as I needed water but the more they would fight the less I'd see him. Then on them rare occasions that I'd see him I couldn't find the words I needed to say to this strange man.

As I became more and more insecure two things took place that likely changed my course for good. I stopped wanting to be a hero when my friends and I would play cops and robbers. I lost all interest in doing the horrible job of being a fireman. The sound of the trucks no longer fascinated me I couldn't stand to hear it anymore. My friends and I would fight over who would be the villains we all wanted to be the bad guys. I don't know if they had the same kinds of issues in their homes that I had in mines but we all ended up on the same path later on in life. What I know for certain is from that young age I lost hope; I lost faith, and I lost my dream.

The second significant thing that took place is my mother started to move around a lot. We'd live somewhere for several months I'd meet new friends and as soon as I was settling in it was time to go. We moved countless times. We moved so... much I couldn't even begin to recall which place we moved in first. It's just one big blur of moves. We lived in every neighborhood in buffalo. We lived in Philly for a few months with one of my aunts. Then one day my mother woke me up screaming. She was on the bed and there was a baby mouse stuck inside a small waste basket. He couldn't get out he was struggling trying to get out with no success. we were stuck on the bed for at least an hour. Her fear made me scared and to this day I jump on beds if I see mice. After about an hour or more my mother realized if we didn't move we'd be stuck until my aunt came home. So she worked up the nerve to ease out of the bed grab a few items and make a run for it out the door. We never looked back and that was the end of Philly for us.

This was my life; it was unstable, and the little things "literally" would have us on the move again. We would always end up back at 85 Landon St. it was the only place I could ever really call home. We had pit stops where we lived for days, weeks or even months in Washington DC.; Baltimore MD., Atlanta GA., Richmond VA., Camden NJ., and in between we'd end up back at 85 Landon.

My mother was mostly all that was certain that my father was very passive when it came to being in my life. It was her way or no way. That meant that she had full control to do two things, torture my father and condition me to believe that he was no good bastard that did wrong. Again I had my own issues with him combined with hers I started to hate my father. I started to blame him for why everything was wrong in my life. I started to act out in every possible way. I became a class clown in school. I'd rush to finish my school work so I could acta fool in class.

This was the period where the change that had been festering in me took place. I was never really a problem child up to this point. I had kept my bad acts under wraps. With a few exceptions here or there of bad behaviors. I would listen to my mother and do what I was told. I had good grades and good manners. I was quiet and shy. In fact I would have to run home from school #53 everyday because this kid Walter used to bully me and promised to beat me up after school. Walter was one of those kids that were big for his age and looked like a little version of Mike Tyson. I would run home and have to keep it a secret because my mother would kick my butt if she ever found out I ran from anyone. She had strict rules: you never run even if the person is bigger than you, pick up something but always defend yourself.

So becoming the class clown, talking out of turn, and being disruptive was all new to me. One day I remember coming to school with a plan to beat Walter silly. I got me some brass knuckles and after school instead of me running home I walked toward the back of the school. Like he always did he followed me talking about what he was going to do to me. As I walked I slipped my hand in my book bag to get my weapon. It was time to settle the score with him. We got to the back of school #53 and he said "now I got you". I turned around had my brass knuckles on and said "let's go". When he saw there was no fear and I was prepared to fight he backed off like the coward that bullies usually are.

At this point I was ready for whatever. I wanted to fight anyone now. I had just punked off the one person in school in I was afraid of. From then on I was a fighter. I started to get into fights with anyone and found out I was good at it too. Which only encouraged me more. I started to become a problem at home. I went from my mother's respectful, smart and handsome boy, to this demon child. This was a sign but it was missed.

I would do the craziest things and my mother would beat me silly. Then call my father curse him out and make him do the same. At first I felt betrayed by her calling this stranger to come beat me. After a while I became numb to it. I just wanted it over so I could get on with my day. His beatings had no substance. So what he was upset or disappointed in me who was he anyway? I felt like he didn't care about my feelings. The beatings from him felt like abuse not love, concern or discipline, just abuse! After all he never stopped to try and figure out why I was acting this way.

This made me angry, it made me despise him, and every time my mother would call him I felt betrayed. I thought it was (us) against the world 'especially' him. He was the enemy, he was the reason we were moving from house to house. I even blamed him for the abuse I suffered at the hands of my sick and twisted cousin. Why was she calling him and why did he only come around for birthdays, holidays, or to beat me?

....

I remember we moved again. My mom thought another move would do the trick, get me away from my friends again. Force me to meet new people that soon as I got to know I'd have to move away from again. I was angry and had no intentions of embracing a new school or new friends. I planned to make life hell for my mom until we moved back home which we did but not before I met my future wife.

I was upset that I was away from home and I had a chip on my shoulder I had a million emotions I was dealing with that I didn't understand but it was in this madness that I remember first laying eyes on my wife. She was probably nine years old. I was eight but first day I was in awe of her. She was such a lady. Unlike any other girl I had ever seen. She was the first girl in a long… time that I had respected and wanted to get to know. From the age of six I had been treating little girls my age or older like objects. I was just trying to get thrills so I could erase the ugly image of my cousin violating my innocence. Then there was Nickie and I wanted to marry her! I barely knew how to spell the word love and I sure didn't know the meaning of it but I knew instinctively that I had it for her.

Sadly I was my shy old self around her. Anytime I was around her I could find no words to speak. I would practice what I'd say to her the next time I saw her. Just like that song that later came out by the group Jodeci "come and talk to me" but I could never get the words out. Then of course we moved again. It really didn't matter because my uncle Steve had a record shop around the corner from where she stayed so I'd have an excuse to be over there.

My uncle Steve, who in reality is my mother's first cousin. He was the son of my Granny Love's sister aunt Tilly who died when I was young. All I really remember about Aunt Tilly is that she was a Diva. She worked hard and she played even harder. She was a rabbit fur and mink kind of woman. She is who my mother got her sense of style from. Steve and his sister May (the cousin's house with all the kids loved to go over) was left alone at an early age. Their mother died when the two of them were grown. They were both in their early twenties. Steve being the youngest of the two at about twenty years old if not younger. The reason I call Steve my uncle is because after his mother died my Granny Love is the one who looked after him. He and my mother always treated each other like siblings.

When his mother died she left her children all her valuables; her car, a little cash and her expensive furs. After her funeral was over and the dust had settled the kids had no money and a car they could hardly afford to put gas in. so my mother came up with this plan with Steve. They would stage the car being stolen then burned up to collect the insurance money. They successfully accomplished this they got the money and Steve went from a young unaware man to a drug dealer. With the help of my mother he was introduced to the right people and became one of the biggest drug dealers in Buffalo. What he also became was my role model.

At this time it was a blur of tragedy for me. I lost my aunt then I lost my illusion of who my mother was. By the second she was becoming all together someone else. On top of this my cousin Antwuan, who was a year older than me died in a house fire. He was one of my running partners. Him, my other cousin Ponny, who was a little younger than me, my friend Jason, and Ant Man. This was my crew than Antwuan died. All of this was in my head on those first days when I met Nickie and I lost my voice. I could talk to my friends and to my little cousins they were safe. All we talked about was sports, games, and things like that. When it came to anything more than that it became difficult for me to speak and Nickie was for sure more than a trivial subject for me.

The thing was after my parents separated my mother began to get deep into dating and she just date any kind of guy. She had a type. The men were all the kinds that shouldn't be around a child. they all fell in one specific category unavailable secure. After my father my mother became unavailable herself. She was more callous her heart was still with my father and she was hell bent on never being hurt again. This made her choose to deal with men for one reason and one reason only to see what she could get from them.

This exposed me to many other harsh realities. She started to do things that made it easy for me to misuse people especially females. I lost respect for females. I had already been objectifying them out of my own pain but now it was easier based on the actions of my mother. My mother became cold and calculated towards men. I can remember when we lived on Nevada St in Buffalo, NY and she moved the refrigerator or stove and how was she going to feed her son? These men all gave her money to buy the appliances then she had these items the welfare paid for brought back into the house. She kept the cash and I can't recall one of those guys eating one meal made from that stove or getting one cold drink out the refrigerator.

I remember another time after we had moved from there and was staying in a house directly behind Granny Love on the street over on Riley. It was early in the morning and my mother had company. This man named Ron came by the house. I didn't know it but my parents were still messing around with each other. I let my dad in and he caught my mother in bed sleep with Ron. My dad was furious, he started beating the man. He was naked and my father beat him all the way out the house. The man went running down the street to his own house naked and my father turned his violent rage on my mother. I ran through the yard to my Granny Love house to tell someone what was going on. I then used that as an excuse to stay at my Granny Love house.

....

With all this madness going on I was a mess and even though my young little heart stirred when I met Nickie. There was no way I could find the words necessary to express these feelings. I would go around her but each time I'd lose the nerve to speak and she started to become insecure around me. She thought I didn't like her and instead of childhood sweethearts we became distant towards each other.

I was almost nine years old. I was in love in my head with this girl I couldn't even say hi to her. I was mourning the loss of family members as well as illusions I had of my mother. I could be anything in life all I needed to do was overcome my rough start. The thing is I can be honest with you as well as myself. By this point I had lost my will. I was on a course to take a long and hurtful journey through life.

Derrel Moore
Confessions Of The Accused

Chapter Four: My First Love Affair

It would be nice if I could say it was Nickie. If it would've been that simple my life would've likely had a much different path. However Nickie was only a wish for many years. My reality was much darker. My first love and one who's broken my heart countless times was money. I fell madly and deeply in love with it and the power attached to it at a very young age.

As I stated my uncle Steve with the assistance of my mother became very... successful in his life as a drug dealer. Partly because his real name was Steve Austin like the tv star and partly because of his status in the streets. The police called him the Six Million Dollar man. I didn't know the character from tv the only Steve Austin I knew and loved was the one with huge rolls of cash, the bulky expensive jewelry, and shiny white car. This man demanded everyone's attention when he was around. Men and women alike would beg to be noticed by him or to have a word with him. Steve was about 5"8 inches in height, maybe 190 lbs., with a shorter length gherry curl. He had this memorable smile with a chipped front tooth. To those that knew him he was amazing but to many he was even more and to me, well he became a god.

Steve owned a record store in the city of Buffalo. It was on E. Ferry St at first, due to him never having a job he had to put the record shop in a cousin of ours and a girlfriends names. So the original name was J & E's for Jennifer (Steve girlfriend) and Eric our cousin. Eric soon wanted out. He saw the record store as a drug front so the name changed but the game stayed the same.

Before long the record store became a main attraction for; family, friends, about two or three real customers, and countless drug deals gone unnoticed due to the mixture of countless traffic. This became my hangout and I got to see up close more of the things I only got a glimpse of at home. I fell deep in love and there was no turning back for me. My destiny became very clear to me. I wanted this life for myself. I started taking notes. I was long ago done with being a kid anyways. I was simply waiting for my moment.

The problem was I was just a kid only about nine so I had some growing to do as well as learning and I was determined to learn. There were many days that some of Steve's kids and I (he had a lot of kids) would stay at his house he had with Jennifer. We would have lots of fun. It was a big clubhouse and never much supervision. Just kids watching kids. On one of those many occasions one of Steve's sons told me and a few of his brothers that he knew the combination to Steve's safe. We were curious to see what was inside so we went in the room got the safe open and was amazed by the sight.

His sons didn't really know what they were looking at. They knew it was drugs but not much else. for me this was like home. I've seen this from a very young age only this time it wasn't a fascinating game. This was my future I wanted to have a safe like this. I wanted what was inside. Then I came up with the idea to take some of the weed so we could sell it. The brothers thought I was crazy but I had ideas. I had been paying attention and waiting on my time to come. So we stole some. It was filled with the stuff we had no idea of its value and I only had an instinctive idea not reasonable one. but I was determined to be loved like Steve. I wanted and needed that power at all costs so I ran into the game on instinct at nine.

Our chance to become drug dealers didn't take long, I told the brothers about these females that were always around. I know Steve will give them weed I had no idea for how much or anything, honestly I just had a feeling could get them to buy it from us and keep it a secret. I was I was right. One day I called them on the phone and I told them "I had what they wanted" I know we sounded very stupid, and we were. The thing was we were Steve's boys, his nephew and sons they told us to come by the house my cousin were scared but it was my destiny. I had no choice, so we went, when they saw I was serious I made my first drug deal. I'm pretty sure they beat us, and they continued to beat us for weeks, but the way they called us handsome, flirting with us treating us like we were grown men. It reminded me of how I saw Steve being treated every single day I had to have this life, I couldn't live without it. I was in love. We were young stupid kids it didn't take long for our operation to get shut down. Somehow we'd gotten sloppy with going in Steve's room to get more weed, and he became suspicious. The problem was, like I said he had a lot of kids, in fact to this day no one really knows how many. The last known count was 33 but no one actually knows. As a result he told all of us that he found out who was going in his room none of us were allowed over. We lost our ability to get our hands on more product and our growing clientele. By the time he let up on his restrictions it was too late and his safe was no longer valuable to us. In fact we went inside and it was empty, we never found anything in it again besides pictures he didn't want anyone to see. We got some cheap perverted thrills off of that but not much else.

This disappointed us, we were counting on that being available and now it was gone. For my cousins it wasn't a big deal as for me I was heartbroken. They found other ways to get things, I would tag along but I wasn't into stealing, it just wasn't really my thing. The truth was I was a pretty spoiled kid, if I wanted something I could have it and so could they. What I really wanted was to be like Steve, I wanted that power, that adoration, and you don't get that from shoplifting! I was heartbroken, I had to have this thing that I did not yet understand, and I just knew I needed it to live.

The sad reality about this kind of god like adoration, the fast money, the cars, trucks, jewelry and all kinds of beautiful women at your beck and call is that the price is high, not just for you but also for those that love you. As men we aspire to be gods and adored as such. But we lack the foresight to see all that comes with such weighty responsibility, especially when your road to reach such heights is illegal, and void of lasting security.

I got to see first up close and very personal, it was Christmas Eve 1989 and I was at my Granny Love house, it was a beautiful time of year. Steve came to the house, it had to be almost 10:00pm. I'll never forget this night... he came in, only for a minute his pearl white pathfinder was still running in front of the house, loud music playing from inside. It was low but you could still hear it you'd know Steve was on his way over when he was blocks away the music was so loud, but not in front of 85 Landon, he'd always turn it down.

After giving my Granny Love a hug, and whatever else he'd stopped to give her, she stopped him in the hall at the threshold of the doorway, "I watched my idol dressed to the nine, jewelry everywhere, looking like Adonis draped in gold". She asked him where he was going, he told her he had to stop by the bar "The Tanqueray", then he was going home. She told him Steve its Christmas Eve, go home that bar will be there tomorrow. Steve said "I know Aunt Sylvie I just need to check on a few things it won't take long". My Granny Love told him "please not tonight I got a feeling just go home to your kids do it another day" she asked him to promise her he'd go straight home and he promised.

Steve went to the Tanqueray instead, some guys tried to kidnap my uncle. Supposedly payback for him not coming to the aid of a woman in his company one day. Because he didn't something happened to her, these men tried to escort him out of the bar. He refused to leave with them, that's when they shot him. Steve subsequently, after months of fighting for his life died. This destroyed our family, and so... many others Steve had kids on the way, two women were pregnant there was so many people that depended on him and at the young age of 31 he was gone. This should have been a life lesson for me, for many of us, instead it only made me angry and more determined.

This lost life placed a void in the lives of many, and someone had to fill that void, this would prove impossible but many tried. He was the reason everyone in Buffalo and other cities knew the Austin name. he was the reason most of us lived dressed and ate good. Bills were paid because of this man, and now he was gone. The irony in this is, I would cause others to experience this same devastation, and it's only as I write these words I'm sorry "even if sincere" is never enough to the love ones of a murder victim.

   Again the void was great, my mother eventually became the person to best to fill that void. She was the person the family looked to for ideas, for some sense of direction, and predictably she failed. The truth is there's simply no way to replace a person, or fill the void left after their death, especially not one of such stature as he was to us.

   The family was going through many forms of grief. There was rage that resulted in acts of retaliation towards people that had nothing to do with his death. Others slipped into denial, and started abusing drugs and the list goes on, and for me I had a mixture of all of these things I was exposed to.

   My mother began to do many things that I observed, and learned from. As she made the adjustment out of anger she was doing all she could to manipulate people to carry out her will, which was to find the people responsible for his death, and make sure they paid the ultimate price for it. She also started to sell drugs more openly, exposing me to it even more, and at the same time she spoiled me rotten with things, no matter what I did wrong. The period between my first drug sale, when Steve was killed, and my mother's crowning, "so to speak" was less than two years. For a child two years is a lifetime, especially one rushing to grow up, and I was in a rush more than ever now that my role model was deceased. So it was no real shock that at eleven I was doing all I could to break into the business.

   I would do almost anything to get my hands on some drugs to take in the streets to sell. I would steal my mother's cocaine, and take it to the neighborhood drug boys. I would sell to them, take whatever price they'd offer me for the stuff. They loved to see me coming because they knew I had no idea what I had. In all honesty I was just satisfied with how they ran to me, and treated me like I was important I felt like the man, and in away the money was only one element of what I wanted, I wanted this feeling that came with the money.

My mother would find out I was outstanding on corners with drug dealers, and she'd beat me like there was no tomorrow. She'd call my father, and they'd take turns beating me. There was no stopping me, I'd take my beating, and wait for her to let me off my punishment, and then I was right back at it. She tried putting me on probation, made threats that she'd send me to a group home for troubled youth. I called her bluff, and she didn't have the heart to put her little boy in the system.

Then we moved, she always thought moving would fix her problems, and just like all the other times, it didn't. I was sent to school in the south Buffalo called south side, and I met another kid that was like me in so many ways. He was about a year older than me, and he had a similar living situation. His pop's was big time drug dealer, and he was a troubled kid. He wanted to do what his pop's did and unlike me, he wasn't being discouraged at home.

This was great for me, I found a person I could hang with that my mom would think was safe. She had no idea who his parent's was, she was just happy I wasn't trying to sneak to cold spring every day. She couldn't imagine that the first friend I'd find would be the son of a major drug dealer that actually had no problem with us selling drugs. She didn't understand, this was my destiny, and there was nothing, or any one capable of getting in the way of it.

My new friend Mone and I started going straight from school to Strauss and Sycamore to sell crack cocaine every day. I would help in the sales and learn the real value of the drugs. I made a few dollars, but it wasn't the money I would get that kept me coming back, it was the knowledge and it was priceless. It was fun while it lasted, it didn't take long for my mother to realize the truth, after all she was in the game herself, and knew almost all the major players. I was banned from Strauss and Sycamore quick she made sure of that. The problem was, it wasn't where I went, or who I hung out with, the problem was in me, and she never realized it until it was too late, to change the course.

My mother was in denial, she thought there was no way I possibly could have remembered, or even been able to understand the things I was exposed to as a child. I mean, I'd been playing on garbage bags of weed at the age of 5 years old like it was a bean bag. She thought I believed it was actually an bean bag the lies we tell ourselves to rationalize our actions are amazing.

I mean I was 9 or 10 years old watching her distribute vacuum sealed ounce packs of cocaine to be sold for her. She allowed herself to believe I actually didn't understand it, the truth is I not only understood, I was falling head over heels in love with the lifestyle, so she could have moved us to Africa, I wasn't going there without my heart, and my heart's biggest desire had gone from wanting to be a fireman, to needing to become the next major drug dealer of the family. There simply was no one in my life capable of stopping me.

CONFESSIONS OF THE ACCUSED

CHAPTER FIVE

MY COMING OUT PARTY

I can clearly remember, it was 1991, I was a little more than a month away from my 13th birthday it was June, the end of the school year, and I felt beyond ready. I was tired of being a kid, an pretending I will grow up to be anything remotely close to what I dreamed up for myself when I was a naive child.

I will never forget it, I had fifty dollars to my name, and I had actually stole the money the night before out of the purse of one of my Granny Love's friends that was visiting with her. They blamed everyone but me, to my Granny Love I could simply do no wrong, and no one dared suggest otherwise to her at the time.

I left early the next morning supposedly to go to school, by then I was in an alternative school for troubled kids. I left determined to never come home, at least not as a child, or as a resident. I left with only the clothes on my back, and the stolen $50. I was looking to find a way into the drug game, and to become the next godlike figure of the streets of Buffalo New York. All I could think of how I'd get jewelry and cars like I've seen the other drug dealers with, especially Steve.

I got about a block and a half away before I started to get a bit scared. I didn't know where I was going nor what my next move was. At this point I have never purchased a drug, I had only stolen drugs, sold drugs with a friend, but this was different and the stakes were much higher. I was now homeless, no food, no clothes, nothing and no clue how I'd change this new self-made reality.

I was walking up the street in my old cold spring neighborhood called Wohler's, this kid I casually knew named Shamel was sitting on the porch, as I approached I could tell he was upset "what up Mel, you aren't going to school"? and he told me "hell no, my mom won't buy me no new sneakers and my birthday coming up", and he went on about his dissatisfactions. This immediately gave me an ally that I could talk to. So I told him "I'm not going either, I'm trying to get this money, forget school". I told him my plans, and he had some of the missing ingredients. I wanted into the crack game, but had no reliable resources.

While I had resources to purchase some drugs, he knew a source that we could get them for the little bit of money I had. It was just my luck (so I thought then), these guys in the neighborhood were selling double-ups, which meant they would sell you drugs worth double your money. As soon as he told me we both went to this drug house, and got a double-up. I gave Shamel half he was now my partner, we went and basically chased down clientele.

We took that long walk to get double ups all day while kids were in school, and by three o'clock when kids where coming from school we had made enough money to stop buying double ups, we moved up the ladder, and we were able to buy eight balls of cocaine. We needed a new connect, and Shamel knew just the person, so we got his beeper number, called him and in the matter of minutes we had one eight ball each, plus Shamel was able to go to the sneaker store called Rick's to purchase new sneakers. We were hooked, it was easy, and there was simply no turning back for us. I often look back, and wonder who was more addicted, the fiend's we sold to, or the fiend's they purchased from. The answer isn't a simple one, either one has its legitimate points, all I know is nothing could've stopped me after that first day I was officially a full blown drug dealer and I was addicted.

Day turned into night, we'd been selling drugs for hours on top of hours, and now my reality was upon me, I have no place to stay. I had left home early that morning knowing I wouldn't return, but not knowing how to make sure of it.

When I look back, it was pretty stupid, and the truth is, I was a twelve year old kid, not only was my actions stupid, they were very telling. The thing is no one knew how to identify what these actions were revealing. After all I was born to children, dead smack in the middle of one of America's worse neighborhoods. I didn't stand a chance of being noticed, and rescued from my own actions that were rooted in pain, as well as fear. This is the thig in the ghetto, as we call it, we're not born with the luxury of being allowed to develop in a so called normal, healthy manner. I know in society as a whole, boys are told not to cry, to suck it up, and not cry like a little girl. This is a societal issue that needs to be addressed. However, couple this with an environment where there's a thousand others added issues, such as lack of education of the parents, the extended family, and most of the people in the child's environment. The extreme poverty, drug abuse, alcoholism, exposure to domestic violence and other adult behavior not suitable to a child, these dynamics will make it impossible for a child of 12, or any age to be noticed as having issues that need professional help, and even if noticed, the resources available to such troubled youth in the hood has its limits.

In the hood, if you start showing signs as I did you're kicked out of school just as I was, then placed in an environment with hundreds of other troubled kids such as alternative schools, group homes if you weren't so lucky. This leads to the next step, supervision by a probation officer, and now your well on the road to your criminal career. There's no room or resources available to deal with the troubled youth in the hood. The fact of the matter is, there's so many, and so little people available that care. Which causes the majority to simply end up criminals/addicts opposed to high school or college graduates. For me I didn't even graduate 8th grade, let alone high school.

It was under these conditions that I found myself in June of 1991, at

12 years old with a drug dealers knot of money in my pocket that I had no idea how to manage, and another pocket full of crack cocaine with no place to call home, even though in my twelve year old heart of hearts 85 Landon street was deeply rooted and would've done anything to go there.

   However, my new found best friend told his mother he wanted me to spend the night. She asked all the questions a mother should, stated the obvious fact of it being a school night, and we told her every lie we could think up. She looked at us with that knowing look, she knew I was in the streets and, I should be at home, but she also knew I wouldn't go, and before she'd let me live in the streets she'd rather me be somewhere safe. I fell in love with her that day, and I started calling her "Ma Duke" she became my other mother, and I've loved her as one ever since.

   Ma Duke was pretty cool, I would send her to Canada bingo almost every day, and she'd go enjoy herself and even win big. She didn't let us know how big, and all we'd get is a pizza party treat, but it was always love. Before long I was there often, some days I'd stay, others I would be out in the streets, I had a goal after all so I was often chasing down money and street fame.

   The other side of this story is more complex, as well as painful. I left home to go to school, and didn't return, I wasn't from a family void of love in fact my family loved me to death. At the time I was living with my Granny Love, my mother was also, so my family was going crazy looking for me and I didn't call or leave a note, I just left.

   Somehow days had past and my family learned where I was and what I was up to. It wasn't like I ran far, I was only around the corner and a few blocks up Wohler's street in between Kingsley and Northampton. My mother unlike past situations with me decided to take a different approach. I believe she finally felt that she had exposed me to way too much, and she could've tried to discipline me, or create a new dynamic to our relationship. Had she tried to discipline me as she had done in the past I think she would've prolonged my progression in the streets. However she was truly without the proper tools necessary to prevent that progression. She was wise enough or had the intuition to recognize this a new dynamic was created.

One afternoon I can remember standing on the corner of Wohler's and Northampton and out of nowhere this 5 foot nothing ball of fire was upon me. My mother scared the heck out of me, my heart was pounding and I just knew I was in serious trouble. As I reflected back a part of me was waiting to be rescued by her. I needed her to come save me from my madness and here she stood. I was terrified and happy at the same time, this lady was my true hero and I missed her.

Instead of popping me upside the head as I expected, and rightfully deserved the way I disappeared, no doubt breaking her heart. However she immediately said "don't worry I'm not going to hurt you, I should but I'm not". Then after easing my mind she rocked me worse with words than she could with her hands. She told me I looked like a prostitute standing on the corner, asked who I was selling myself for and as I tried to protest she cut me off with words I'll never forget "I know I showed you this life, it isn't your fault it's mines and I may not be able to get you to stop because it's what I showed you, but please come home tonight so I can talk to you and show you a better way". I told her I'd come to the house, she looked at me, then said "Dee please come by the house if you going live this life you need to do it right, you look like a hoe out here and you come from better than this", I promised I'd come, she had my attention. That day she had embarrassed me in front of my drug dealing peeps, but more than that she destroyed any hope that there would be any saving. This was my life and not even my own mother was trying to stop me anymore. That day I'd felt like I won, but over two decades later I know it was that very moment that I had lost.

That night I went to my Granny Love house, I waited until it was late because I knew my Granny Love would be upstairs in bed with my granddad before I went. I lightly tapped on the window, my mother was up and she was waiting.

The two of us were a bit uneasy seeing as the dynamics of our relationship was about to change. I was weeks away from my 13th birthday, yet I was there to speak with her about how to be a better drug dealer. How to survive in the life it was my own mother who was about to give me her latest lessons. She wasn't about to teach me how to do a math problem or how to treat my first girlfriend she was about to do her best to give me the tools to survive in the life that she felt hopeless in keeping me from, she was about to do her best in her mind to save my life.

I can imagine you the reader trying to judge her, those in my family may be upset for my candid revelations, and some will stand to dispute it and fight for which you don't know, and for those of you that want me to water down this truth, if we could afford to any longer I'd be glad to but there's too much and too many who need saving. I can't hide at their expense and you can't expect me to.

The thing is, in the hood we have many secrets and our youth have been the price we've paid in order to keep these secrets. the facts are that our youth are being prepared to fail and instructed on exactly how to fail at high level. What does a child with a child do wen it's time to parent? What happens when that child's child starts to have psychological issues from traumas that parents doesn't understand. Let's go back a bit, what happens when the parent of that child that's still a child starts to have these issues at the same time, or in the process of having this baby? Who teaches the child? If the people with these duties have limited education, no medical coverage, living in poverty and also dealing with a thousand other issues that appear to be more important in the moment, whom or what is left to deal with this?

It's always easiest to judge but when it's time to roll up your sleeves and put in the work to make a difference this is when the loud, opinionated messes run for cover. The truth is the solutions are as complex as the issues and for many it's easier just to judge and move on. This is why our prisons are growing and our schools are shrinking.

That night my mother gave m what she had, and if she didn't instead of me writing this story I would be at least 20 years into my grave. She didn't choose the best course, not because she didn't love me or want the best for me, the best was just unavailable to her, therefore making it unavailable for her to give to me, so she gave me what she had and my road was rough, it wasn't ideal but unlike so many of my peers what little she had helped me survive, and I'll forever be grateful that she didn't allow her pain, disappointment and shame to make her run, hide and quit on me.

There's a great deal of mothers out here faced with the same dilemma with even less to offer their own children and as a result the news station is filled with stories of our dead. Our children are dying at an all-time high and coming to prison as if it's an amusement park. This has to be addressed in a more effective way. We have to do better as a society, however we first have to know better.

I left the next day after staying up in the late hours of the night, my mother told me her pain, her mistakes and let me know she didn't want this life for me, however she said she knew her son and instead of playing a fool, living in denial she'd help introduce me to someone that could help me get to where I wanted to be without having to make all the typical mistakes as most people, and end up in prison, she was true to her word, I just failed to listen to her instructions. I was a hard headed kid after all. Nothing she could say or do with the tools she had was capable of changing the course I was on, and I was on a deadly one.

In the coming days I became bold, I was aggressive and determined to own my moment. My mother had given me instructions and told me to stay off the corners making myself an easy target for police and stick up boys looking to rob dudes they catch slipping. I took all her words to heart and I started forcing my way into other people's established space. I became a bully in my approach and it was working which only encouraged me even more.

I remember one day one of my older cousin's friend told me I couldn't

sell drugs at his drug spot. He told me I was blocking his customers and told me I had to go. I went to the gas station, got some gas and created a Molotov cocktail and threw it through the window. If I couldn't sell my stuff there, then no one could! I had to make sure my point was made with more than words. I wanted everybody to know,
Lil Dee wasn't the little kid they were used to treating me like. I wasn't just one of them either, I planned to earn mines one way or the other.

After that incident I was the talk all over the neighborhood and to some it was funny but others were scared. They didn't know what was next or how to treat me, so they avoided me or befriended me. The guy who girlfriend's house it was, that was dealing out of it went and told my grandmother. My Granny Love didn't believe him, and she told me about what he said which upset me. My Granny Love was off limits to the reality of my actions in the streets. I told him that better be his last time talking my business to her, and I meant that. He would cross me again and learn just how seriously I'd lost my way.

CONFESSIONS OF THE ACCUSED

CHAPTER SIX

TRUE TO HER WORD

As I stated, my mother hadn't just promised to teach me things, she also promised to provide certain resources and she did. I was weeks removed from the night we'd spent talking and I'd stayed clear of that corner she'd found me on. I was finding other ways to make money and it also added a security element to it by not being exposed like that.

Then out of nowhere, a guy I'd seen around that lived right in the area stopped his car in front of me. It was a gold BMW, which he rarely drove. He would usually be in his old, bent up looking car, I didn't think the BMW was his because there would be no reason to ride in that beat up car if you owned that. Again, I was young and I was learning on the job.

This strange man asked me was I "Lil Dee", Darlene's son and I told him yeah. He told me to get in, he wanted to talk to me. I initially refused, until he convinced me he was doing her a favor. I got in, he drove in silence for a moment, I'm sure it was calculated. Then the real lessons started to take place, by example, this man showed me the art of the game I was in and knew absolutely nothing about from the ground up.

He taught me over the course of the next few weeks many things, and over the years from thirteen until well after the arrest, three and a half years later. taught me many more, it wasn't just about selling drugs either, he was teaching me how to be a man among the boys in the life I had chosen.

I refuse to say his name, I wouldn't want to bring any harm on him by attracting attention to him. He always worked very hard avoiding attention, and I won't violate that boundary. I can say for certain that besides god, and my mother this man is the only other person I can credit for me walking away from that game with my life despite all the odds.

I didn't know exactly why my mother told this man, or what influence she had that got him to take such an interest in me. I had never seen him around our family or her, he wasn't a well-known dealer to me, in fact I used to see him and had no ideas he sold drugs at all.

This man was a mystery and he was offering me the easy expressway into the upper levels of the game. His only requirement was that I did it right, which strangely was my mothers new requirement. He paid someone to teach me the chemistry of the drug I was selling. He actually gave me drugs, told me to have this lady he sent me to, to cook it up into crack for me. Unknown to me at the time, he paid her in advance to beat me out the drugs. When I came back to him complaining that what he gave me was no good, he took me back and had her show me what she'd done to beat me. Then told her to teach me how to do it myself and never be beaten again.

At thirteen I was no longer in school, at least not the one I needed to be in. He had me in a new school and I was well on my way. I was a fast learner and before long I knew how to do every possible thing with cocaine. The thing is, I was a child and I had no business in this life at all and it should've been predictable that I'd make plenty poor choices.

I wasn't satisfied with learning the very valuable lessons I was learning. Plus I was too young, stupid, and short sighted to become exactly what my heart desired. So I was in the streets making a name for myself in many ways that was counterproductive to my goals and actually went against the things I was being shown.

Remember my mother had embarrassed me and said I looked like a prostitute on the corner, and asked me who I was selling myself for. This had stuck in my head and when other low level drug dealers would offer me drugs to sell for them I would feel disrespected. This would cause me to accept their drugs but not pay them their money. For the most part I got away with doing this, they'd take the loss and not deal with me anymore. I thought I was tough, the truth was altogether different and I had no idea my actions were hurting me more than them.

My actions would eventually catch up with me one way or another and most of them were smart enough to realize that and there was no use starting a feud of any kind with someone with less to lose than them. So I got a pass, however I got bolder and eventually did it to someone that didn't walk away which caused me attention that my mentor didn't want at all. This dramatically slowed down our interaction, hurting me more than I gained by not paying a low level dealer his money. I told him I would and if I couldn't keep my word on a two hundred dollar agreement, how could I be trusted on something major? I didn't think that far and it cost me.

I got put on the burn by my mentor and he wouldn't deal with me the same for awhile, I started to lose focus a little. I was still dealing, I just started to mix business with pleasure. This allowed major distractions to occur and money to be wasted. I started to have a lot of female attention, more than I could handle and drama followed.

My girlfriend at the time stayed in the langfield apartments, she would pop up out of no where and this would cause me all kinds of problems. I would have to run and hide and Shamel would have to cover for me and get rid of the hang arounds or tell my girlfriend I wasn't around. This caused many problems for me at thirteen that I vowed to correct. However it would take me being devastated by one of my hang arounds to really inspire me to snap out of this form of child's play.

I had this one girl that would always be in the neighborhood visiting her friend, we took a liking to each other, and she was about eighteen years old, her name was Robin. She got a caramel skin tone, with a very voluptuous video girl body. I liked her, and although I was thirteen she was into me as well, of course I lied about my age. I t didn't take long before we were having sex every time we seen each other anywhere that we felt the urge. One time I was walking her to her house and we ended up on the side of a church on Utica and Welker. We were in the middle of doing what young kids do that are too hot to think and we realized where we were, so we reluctantly stopped.

The way we carried on it was no surprise she ended up pregnant. I was surprised, way too stupid to be scared but she wasn't, she already had two kids, and on top of that she wasn't a fool she'd noticed how I'd run when my girlfriend would show up. So, she started asking me all the tough questions a mother of two kids knows to ask and I had none of the answers she wanted to hear. She told me she wasn't going to have more kids by a guy who wouldn't be around in the kid's life. I made every promise that I'd take care of my kids no matter what, as he was expecting to have twins. She insisted that wasn't good enough, asked me would I be with her and would I get out of the streets. At that age I was foolish, bold and had very few words in my vocabulary. There was simply no way I was about to give up the streets, nor settle down, I told her to have my babies and give them to me, they'd be fine. I stopped asking and started demanding, she eventually told me what I wanted to hear, "she'd lived a little I hadn't", and she went behind my back and got the abortion and then had my cousin tell me what happened.

I can't pretend this didn't make my knees buckle because it did, and I was angry. I went looking for her, but it was too late, she knew I was a fool and she wasn't. She was nowhere to be found, I never saw Robin again, and till this day I still think of what I lost.

This pain inspired me to refocus, grow up a bit more, and it also made my heart grow a lot harder. I became ruthless in the streets and avoided the familiar neighborhood for a while, I started to hang around one of my older cousins, one of the shadiest, untrustworthy people you'd ever want to meet. He showed me how to get in real trouble and how to do it without remorse. Let's call him shady to protect his identity.

These actions took me way off the path my mom had set me upon. It would be a long time before I found my way even remotely close to what she had in mind. I was exposed to the harshest realities of the streets, and I fell in love with a new form of power, the power of the gun. It was better than money because money inspired fake friends to show up and it inspires vultures to come hunt for you. Truth is, with money can't tell who is who. Family, friends, and vultures all become one and you become the prey.

With the gun you were both the predator as well as adored. Yes, most only pretended to adore me out of fear, but this was better than pretending out of greed and larceny. Here is where I must not defer, there was no one that forced me on this path, nor fully exposed me to it. I got a glimpse and took to it like water.

As I reflect, the God honest truth I had an angry edge ever since I had allowed myself to be touched by that monster as a child. In my mind it was my own fault, and, in my mind, I planned to never let it happen again. I was determined to protect myself, sadly what I actually did was avoid facing the pain and this put in my most vulnerable position. In my extreme effort not to be victimized ever again, not only did I become a continuous victim, ironically, I become my biggest victimizer. It was my very hands that the most damage was done, I was so hell bent on not being hurt that I hurt others. However, I know best that I hurt no one more than I hurt myself.

I became obsessed with carrying a gun with me no matter what I was doing or where I was. There was even one occasion where my Granny love was on my case and she made me promise to do it so I went to church. I got to the door of the church when I realized I had my gun on me, I couldn't go in there like that. However, it was always in my head that if Steve would have listened to Granny love he would still be alive. So, I always followed her directions and didn't second guess her. With this dilemma I decided to sit on the side doorsteps of the church, listened to the service but I did not enter the house of God with my weapon.

I was so hell bent on having a gun no matter what my reputation became, even to the cops. It got to the point that every time certain cops would see me they would stop me and book me for my gun. I was only thirteen, so they would just take my gun and take me home to my mother or take me to the precinct until she picked me up. She'd always show up for me, always say the right things to the police, and once outside the precinct she'd ask if I was coming home but my answer would always be the same. She would always be heart broken, angry, dejected and beat, however she'd give me advice, she'd love me anyways, and always, she always assured me that she would be here for me.

Many months passed, and I had been hanging in the Doat and Burgard area hustling. I was staying away from my old neighborhood, I had learned from my mother that getting away from by moving away from it was a coping skill. What Robin had done hurt me in many ways, ways that I didn't understand at all. One of the typical signs of a kid who has experienced serious trauma is their strong desire to have a child of their own. It is as if they feel like they get a do over, like they have to prove that there is a better way to raise

And protect a child than the way they had. I didn't recognize why losing my children hurt so much. I just knew it did and I learned to run so I did.

While in that area my cousin took me to meet his new girlfriend Her name was Angie she was beautiful and a sweetheart. I didn't understand then, nor do I understand to this day what she seen in my cousin. Whatever it was she was really into him, and at the time I had to give him his props. By this time, I was fourteen years old, I had been in the streets for well over a year and I guess I looked the part. However close inspection, with sober and better-informed eyes, there was no mistaking the fact that I was still a boy trying to be something I wasn't.

I met Angie's sister that night her name was Star, she was just a beautiful but had a darker edge to her. She was less sophisticated and was raunchier in her speech and actions. I enjoyed the meeting, but I was ready to get back to my sanctuary 'the streets' and had said as much. Star asked me to stay and hang out and she offered me some beer, which she had been drinking heavily. I declined as I didn't drink at all or do any drugs, my addiction was of another kind and it was elusive to fully figure out.

I was a sucker for a pretty face, so she convinced me to stay. I still had zero thoughts of anything being possible between us. I mean she was a grown woman, twenty-two years old, and in my head, she was out of my league. I didn't even consider the thought, before I knew it, drunk out of her mind and aggressive she invited me into her room to have sex. I was nervous, who am I kidding? I was terrified.

All I could think about was I was a kid, I was inadequate, as soon as she seen my penis shed realize I was a little boy, but I still had to do it. I was in the streets and I had been confronting all types of fears worse than this, each time I went in head first. There was no turning back, I wasn't going to tuck in my tail and run home to mommy to let her know I couldn't handle the streets. So just as those times I pretended to be eighteen years old with a lot of experience and I had sex with her. Surprisingly to me she didn't complain we started to see each other. She was aggressive in our sexual encounters as she was in my initial observations and I learned from her on the job.

We eventually became inseparable, I moved in with her and without even noticing it I hadn't been in the streets selling anything. I was caught up, I was learning how to be a man in another way and it was appealing to me. She had two kids a boy and a girl, I fell in love with those kids. I started to live the family life and slowly we settled into it. She even stopped drinking because I didn't do it, nor did I like her to.

Beautiful woman, two beautiful kids and a great sex life, happy ending? I wish, I was a kid there was no way I was done making foolish decisions.

My cousin, the same one I had to thank for meeting her came over and wanted me to go with him and despite her initial protest I went. The night ended with me in custody for a carjacking case. This was a serious felony, no going home to mom this time. This landed me in juvenile, the case even made the newspaper and this lead to Star learning she lived with a fourteen-year-old boy. She was devasted and I was busted in more ways than one.

My precious mother, she was always there, even if I didn't deserve it. She was true to her word and always showed up for me. She not only showed up to court, she also made sure the complainant never came, and the charges were placed on an open calendar in case the victim surfaced, it was over.

The bad news was, Star was upset, and I didn't know how I would face her. I was embarrassed but I also loved her and didn't want to give up the fantasy we'd built. I went home, she had been drinking and he was emotional.

She asked me all kinds of questions, and after the questions we stayed together. The only new dynamic was that she'd talked to my mother and my mother got her to agree to something I didn't like.

I hadn't been to school; the streets were my school and my mother hated it. She could learn to accept some of my actions, but she could never accept me being an uneducated fool. She told Star "if you going to be with him, fine but don't let him become a damn fool, laying under your roof when he should be in school, send him to school". This was crazy my mother had employed my lady to do the very job she'd felt like she lost the rights to.

I agreed, and I was going at first until I realized this isn't what I wanted to do. I started to feel like a kid again and I was broke. I was being taken care of by Star and her baby's father, I couldn't live like this. I had to make something happen for myself, and my mother was always true to her word.

I went to see her and told her I was broke and that I needed help, she cursed me out and asked me why I hadn't kept in touch with my mentor that she'd sent to me. I had no excuse, it was pride and pride always shows its ugly face before the fall. My mother was very upset, it was one thing to accept your son is doing certain things, it was even okay in her mind that she'd indirectly aided my actions. However, I was now asking her to go beyond this, I was asking that she remove any delusions she had created in order for her to sleep at night. I wanted her to give me the actual drugs I needed to get on my feet, and she was dying on the inside, but I was too ignorant to recognize this, or I didn't care enough to. She gave me cash, she said she didn't care what I did with it, it was on me, but she wasn't going to give me any drugs.

We both knew it was a lie and shed given me drug money, she wasn't foolish enough to think that I wasn't about to take it and go buy my own. I was back, and instead of going to school I went to the Doat and Burgard area to sell drugs and I was hiding what I was doing from Star like he was my mother. The high that comes from selling the drug soon consumed me and before long I wasn't home much.

Star thought I was cheating, she was on my case and we no longer had the fantasy, it was arguments and soon she started to escalate to confrontations. I had been taught well to never hit a woman regardless of the circumstances and despite having witnessed my father beating my mother. I refused to adopt that ugly characteristic from him, besides I was with a woman with a predisposition to physically communicate her displeasure. When I would come home she would smell me and if I smelled weird it would be a problem, the fact of the matter was that I wasn't cheating, truthfully, I was trying to get myself back on track and reach my goal. I had lost focus being with her, and I was trying to figure out how to be with her without losing myself.

I was doing a poor job and after she punched me in my face for coming in one night with my cousin Ebony's lipstick innocently on me, I started really staying away. Then her, and her sister Angie, the ride or die, two the hard way that they were at the time came looking for me. They came to the block, I was standing on a corner, not listening to the wise words of my mother and Star jumped out on me hitting me like I was one of her prostitutes that ran off. The irony of the situation didn't escape me and my days of standing on corners needed to stop, I had to figure out a better way.

I grew tired of the drama and knew I had to end the relationship. I loved her but at the time I didn't love anything "not even myself", more than I loved all that came with selling drugs. It wasn't easy she actually held me at knife point, trapped me in a corner in our bedroom for a long time telling me I wasn't leaving. Her sister Angie was there, and she convinces Star to let me leave.

I ended up in the streets again, I was staying in the drug house that my cousin, I will call him Q, had with two of his longtime friends. They reluctantly let me become a part of their operation, we all had shifts we worked the house and kept the profits made. They knew I was young, they really didn't want me around because they knew I was bound to cause them trouble but against their better judgement I was a part of the team.

Things were going great, I was making more money than I ever had up to this point. Then this young kid "honestly, we were about the same age", he kept begging to be given drugs to sell but no one would even think of it. He was addicted to playing dice for money and had no interest in anything else, so everyone refused. He started to focus on me, I told him he was too young and that he needed to go to school, stay out of the streets. The whole house laughed, they probably thought it was crazy that I was telling him this when no one could get me to the advice.

To me I was different, this was my destiny and I had no choice in the matter, this was my life. I was trying to make sure he didn't end up making the same mistake I already did. I had no way of knowing at fourteen that my life hadn't even started yet, I had a chance to get it together with the right guidance. I couldn't see this for me, but I was begging him to see it for himself.

He instead told me I wasn't that much older than him, wouldn't leave me alone about it and he broke me down. I said "okay" everyone warned me not to do it, I said "no, I'm going to try you out but if you mess up my money, I'm going to shoot you". He promised he wouldn't have me his word he'd do the right thing. I said " just remember I begged you to go to school and do the right thing, but if you mess up my money I'm going to shoot you, I don't care about your age you want to be in the street and not go to school, I'm going to treat you like a man". He took the ten-dollar bags of crack I gave him and agreed to pay sixty dollars. I told him id give him more when he proved he could do the right thing. Although the speech I gave him was directed at him, the words were more to myself, fear of a child trapped inside the madness that was me. I was just too far gone and there was no one that could get through to me, not even the little boy inside me who wanted to go home and grow up to be a fireman. When the young kid left everyone told me I was stupid and that he wasn't going to pay, to just count it as a loss. I told them without any doubt in my mind that if he played me I would make him wish he went to school. They thought it was a joke and I secretly hoped he wouldn't make me show everyone that I was all out of jokes. I was in the cold harsh streets and I was playing for keeps, I had no intentions of playing games. Play time was over, I didn't have any G.I Joe in my hands, I had crack cocaine and a gun. This was real life and no one, not even the boy in me was about to stand in my way!

The very next day the morning shift was mine and no one was at the drug house but me. The little boy came knocking, I was surprised, I said "I'm glad to see you, you got my money"? he said "Dee I messed up, I need you to give me something else, I had the money, but I started playing dice, I was winning at first but then I lost everything".

I told him "come in' and locked the door behind him and instructed him to take a seat. I was in the house playing a video game, I took the game off pause, continued to play as I berated him. I said "I begged you to go to school, told you this wasn't for you but you didn't listen", he tried to interrupt "no you listen, I told you that you were too young for this, you begged me and promised that you would be able to handle it, I told you to go to school but you refused and when I gave you my shit I told you if you played games, and if you didn't have my money I was going to shoot you". I paused the game, took the 380 handgun out removed the safeties from both trigger, and hammer, as he begun to beg, I pulled the trigger. I shot him in his chest, and his fear, combined with adrenaline caused him to run out the house into the street.

I knew he'd tell what happened and where it happened at, id realized too late that I'd made a mistake. I had to clean up, there were drugs everywhere, I had to get what I could and flee the house quickly, but I didn't know where I'd go, I just ran and ran. I ended up on the train tracks, I hid the gun the triple beam scale and drugs then I went home to my mother, she was always there for me.

I caught a cab to my Granny loves house, where my mother was currently at the time. She knew when she seen me that something was seriously wrong, she took me upstairs and told me to tell her everything. When I hesitated, she said "Boy I'm your mother I'm always going to be on your side but I can't help you if I don't know what happened, you can lie to any and everyone but me, tell me what happened so I'll know how to help you I'm on your side and I won't let anything happen to you"

I told her everything, and it took her seconds to think of her next move. She turned me in to the police! I went kicking and screaming, I just couldn't believe my mother's idea of help was turning me in to the cops! She assured me that it was the only way, she said that boy would tell, and the police would come right to my Granny loves house looking for me. So, she walked me right into the precinct and told them I was the one who accidently shot my friend. She also told them that I ran away scared and that I'd thrown the gun on the train tracks even gave them a fake set of tracks to search for it.

They took me into custody and sent me to east ferry group home with the worst of the worst. By this time, I'd been arrested for three guns and carjacking, I was on my way to be a career criminal. I spent three days there, and after my mother made some calls I was moved to a better place, a place where you'd get to leave and go home, go to the movies on the weekends, it was like a halfway house for troubled youths. I was upset, this wasn't what I had in mind, but my mother kept telling me to trust her, and she'd never given me a reason not to, so I did. I spent eight days in this two-story house, went back to court and was released. I never had to return to court, and only a few people know all the reasons why. I'm not one of them, all I know is that my mother was always true to her word where it concerned me and helping me in my madness. I don't know what her reasons were, I just know she was a better person to me than I was to her.

Honestly when I shot that kid, in a sick twisted way I was shooting myself, my anger, my disappointment, it wasn't about him or the sixty dollars, truthfully, I was trying to kill whatever innocence I still had in me. I was tired of hearing the little boy in me begging to go home, somehow, he needed to die in order for my pain to manifest into the monster I was becoming to live.

Derrel Moore

Confessions Of The Accused

Chapter 7

Now They Fear Me

After that incident I didn't go back to the area where the incident I didn't go back to the area where incident happened, I was back in the Cold Springs, and a lot had changed since I left. For starters the location to make drug money for my crew had changed, the new spot to be was just one street over, on Riley Street. From where my Granny love lived this was a little too close for comfort, plus it was another corner attraction and I didn't like the idea.

At the same time Ma Duke, Shamels mother had been saving money we'd give her, she'd also go to bingo, win and save. She wanted to buy a house, and she actually did it, she took us to see it and it looked like hell on earth, there was no way it would become a place to live. However, she was determined to prove us wrong and teach us a life lesson at the same time. In the meantime, money had to be made, so I had to figure out how to do this with so many changes going on and do it in a way my mother would accept. I would still be on the same block, I just figured I'd be more careful about it, the truth was I was hardheaded and didn't know what good advice was. My first day out on the block, trying to reestablish myself with my customers I played myself and got beat for some packages.

Although this was my neighborhood all my life, I had been gone for months, so I was the new guy on the block. This had me a little anxious, at the same time my older friends had been giving me props, and I had just come from my juvenile jail for a shooting. In the hood, I was the man, the older dudes looked at me differently, and I was gaining more respect.

All these elements had many different emotions going through me when this customer pulled up in a U-Haul truck. Like three people rushed to the truck, all trying to make the sell, there was no order at all, it was every man for himself. I decided to bully my way in on the action, and the customer not recognizing me as being from around there decided to teach me a lesson. He told everyone "I'm going to deal with the young blood right here", referring to me. They walked away, he had a handful of money and he told me to show him what I was working with. So I took out my four biggest ten dollar bags of crack and stuck them in the window to show him. He hit my hand knocking them out, then he drove away.

The entire block started laughing, they clowned me and told me that's exactly what I get, I was on fire, told them to stop playing with me and that next time I seen that fool I was going to kill him. They just laughed and disregarded my words, telling me it was my fault and I should know better. Truth is I did, I wasn't supposed to be on that corner like a two-dollar prostitute, but I had a hard head, I thought I was much smarter than I was.

I started to venture out again, between Shamel and I going on Smith street, where Ma Duke had purchased the house, 'because she would force us to go and help her clean' and trying to locate a new drug house in coldspring. Shamel and I were tired of helping Ma Duke, we were trying to make money not work on a beat-up house. So, we found some crack heads in the area, paid two of them to help her and with the promise to pay them every day we were off the hook. We tried to make money over there, but we didn't know anyone, and ma duke was paying attention. She didn't want that around where she was trying to build her first home, so we would walk around but we had very little success at the time.

I was also dealing with a few other people, trying to put something together, I had stumbled upon something which was great until it fell apart. A good friend from the neighborhood and I found a place on Life Street. The money was good, the set up was great, but then one day my boy got locked up for beating one of his classmates to death. I was devasted, we had so many plans, we were about to do some great things together, then that went down out of nowhere. There was so many rumors as to what happened but all that matters is he was gone, and I was hurt.

I sensed every possible plan was blowing up in my face, I went back on Life a few times, but it wasn't the same, and the vibe seemed off. I ended up back on the corner of Riley and Wohler's truth is this is where my friends were, any excuse would do, and I just needed to be around my friends at any cost.

Things were okay at first until some family from Lackawanna moved on Landon Street, right down the street from my granny love, and started selling drugs out the house. This had everybody upset, not only were they strangers to us, they were selling their drugs for twice as cheap as we were. This was killing our business, and no one liked it, so I came up with a plan, they had to go.

Honestly no one wanted to make a move on them not knowing anything about them, but I was way too stupid to be worried about who they might have connections to. So the night I planned to spray their drug house, some people tried to discourage me, others wanted to see if I had it in me. I was on my way through a short cut to Landon when I spotted a familiar face, the same guy that was in the U-HAUL truck weeks earlier, this was perfect, almost everyone he did it in front of was out there. He pleaded with me, told me he found out I was one of the Austin's and that my mother name was Darlene, and said he gave my money to my cousin. I didn't believe him, my cousin 'the shady one', never told me he got my money, and even if he did get it what about my pride ?! I gave him five seconds to run, as soon as he heard me start to count, he turned to run, and without remorse I shot him.

I didn't stop to think it might prevent me from also being able to get rid of these people in our neighborhood, but it did. I was furious, I wanted to get these people, I didn't know them, don't even know why I was doing it. What I did know was that I was starting to like shooting a gun, not just having one.

It didn't take long until I could get my next fix, the way I felt knowing the power I had was addictive. So when this guy I knew for several years, actually a good friend of my cousin 'shady', disrespected me on the block in front of everyone, there should've been no doubt to what I'd do.

I was only a kid in his eyes, he'd known me since I had snot hanging from my nose, and he used to give me change for the store. He couldn't see past that so he tried treating me like he used to, he was one of the few who hadn't gotten the memo yet and it was time he got it. I went around the corner to his best friend's house, my cousin shady, and got his gun, I didn't tell him who for, and came running back around the corner. It was a summer night, it was beautiful outside and almost everyone was out there, it was perfect.

When he seen me, at first he didn't move, but then he noticed the gun and started to run. I chased him into a yard where he begged me not to shoot him, I aimed for his face and shot. I don't exactly know why, but the bullet hit him in the shoulder as he tried to protect himself, and my cousin the shady one was soon upon me, snatching the gun before I could fire a second shot.

Honestly, I don't know why I wanted to kill him that night, (especially in front of dozens of people). I was on autopilot, there was no reasoning in my brain at all, of any kind. The truth is that man was a friend of my family, yes, he had been disrespectful, he had even told my grandmother I fire bombed his girlfriend's house the year before, and made threats that night to go tell her I was around there but these things were minor, and none warranted his death. Had I been able to reason, this would've been an easy conclusion to reach.

The cerebrum is not developed in the brain of a fourteen-year-old kid, I was living on instincts and operating out of survival mode. In my premature mind he was a threat to the survival of who I was trying to be, to him I could never be more than a snot nosed kid. I had to figure out how to survive his perception of me, and my instincts compelled me to get rid of the problem, I was tired of running from it, tired of being seen as "Lil Dee", I had to destroy that image. Therefore, when this happened, and the street was filled with witnesses I felt this was the best time to kill that man, as well as the perception of Lil Dee. I didn't see witnesses in a court of law out there, I saw witnesses to my becoming more than a boy, and they were there to witness the death of Lil Dee so that my madness could live.

I couldn't see it then, there was no way I could understand that I was doing my best to destroy myself. In my fragile, uninformed mind I believe I was this man that I was acting out, truth is if it was really my nature I wouldn't have had to work so hard trying to convince myself of it. I wouldn't have been forced to shoot my friend, create conflict, and overall destroy my past.

In many ways I got the desired effect, I was no longer Lil Dee, I was crazy. People would call me this with a smile, in an inoffensive tone to my face, but behind my back the meaning and the tone was different. I became the person no one really wanted to be around, but no one dared to say so. Fear was always better than love in the streets, and there was no doubt that I started stirring up some fear.

I didn't bank on this fear showing in family and friends, but it did, I wasn't just killing an image I was killing relationships that I trying to preserve as they were. My best friend, my brother from another mother Shamel was being encouraged by Ma Duke to stay away from me. My reputation was growing by the day as I was working overtime to build it. My brother and friend loved me, but in his heart, he wasn't like me. He didn't have the same drive to destroy his past as me, he wasn't running from the darkness I was.

One day out of nowhere my brother, my one and only friend told me he was moving down to Carolinas with his grandmother. He didn't have the heart to tell me the role I had in this change, but I knew. That June day a few years ago I found him on the steps dissatisfied had changed his life. There was no doubt I played a serious part in that change, and although he hadn't gone as far into the deep end as me, we all knew it was only a matter of time. I was on my own, all I had was a growing reputation, my deeply rooted pain, and everyone was to blame but me, I was a ticking time bomb, and the truth is they had the right to fear me, if I was smart I would've been scared too.

After he left I became a miniature version of what I was as a child, moving from place to place with my mother. I was a bit of everywhere searching to fill a void that had been in existence since I could remember. I had this hardening heart, I was uncertain in life as I had ever been. My father was showing up less and less, I think it's because he didn't want to deal with the reality that his junior was out of control, it was easier to just avoid me. Which made it that much easier for my young heart to grow bitter.

My mother on the other hand, her approach was different, she loved me regardless, and did her best to stay involved and keep communication open with me. When it's really analyzed, it was fear based, my mother, my extended family, my peers, and even myself, it was all fear. I became unapproachable, I became a master of giving the impression that no one or nothing would change me, and fear led everyone to buy the crap I was selling.

In truth, I was a little boy, I don't care how many rugs I sold or how many guns I'd shot, I was a boy. I was still a kid, and deep down all I wanted was some attention. I wanted my parents to recognize my trauma, rescue me, protect and nurture me, I was screaming to be noticed and with each passing day I was broken a bit more. It became easier to pretend, easier to fool those observing me, I became as convincing as any award-winning actor, and this was my academy award performance. Sadly, the award for being so good would be a fate no child should ever have.

Confessions of the accused

Chapter 8

One more chance

Make no mistake my mother was no pushover, she was one of the strongest women I've ever known. In no way do I intend to paint her as a helpless or a pushover, she was far from it. So after she watched me make a mess of my life, and did her best to guide me without alienating me from her. She decided to take a page out of her old book, she decided against my protest that I was moving to Virginia.

She didn't beg, this was the toughest person id ever really encountered, male or female. So I went with her, and I secretly wanted a change. By then I turned fifteen and I hadn't really had the type success in the drug game than I expected. There were more problems (much more), than money involved, I really didn't bank on the problems, and I just wanted the jewelry and cars. By that point I had purchased very little jewelry, none like my idols and I had yet to get close to buying my own car.

I left, we went to Richmond Virginia with one of my mothers' good friends, and her name was Patty. We had close family friends down there, my mother helped this friend to make some valuable connections when he was in Buffalo, which I will not mention, and he was glad to have her come down there to see if she could change my course. He also had a thing for Patty which is why she was with us.

We stayed with his sister, where he had room but didn't stay there. I hated it from the start, there was nowhere for me to go. The one area across the bridge where I'd seen a housing project and basketball court was off limits for me. He told my mother it was a bad area and under no circumstances should I cross that bridge to go there.

This place was calling me, and I was on lockdown, I was ready to go! I had been there for about three days, and I was a very observant kid, so I noticed that my mother's would go to the room he has, which was locked, each time he came over. He'd go in alone, no one else could go inside and he would always lock it back up, he wouldn't use the bathroom with that door unlocked. My instincts told me that there was something in there.

The next few days passed, and I was waiting to get my chance to have a look inside. My chance came when he took my mother and Patty out on the town. I immediately went upstairs to work on the door as everyone downstairs was sleep, the lock was too hard to manipulate without damaging the door, I was going to give up, I didn't want to damage the door and find out there wasn't anything in there. So I went and laid down, I thought about the type of business he was in while in Buffalo, my mind was made up.

I went back to the door knowing there was no way I wasn't getting in, there was no doubt in my mind that there was something worth having in that room. I forced the door open without even trying to prevent damage to the door, I listened for people downstairs, no movement, and I went in. I found the light and was immediately disappointed. It was a room full of what appeared to be junk, there was no order and the room appeared to be filled with worthless old junk furniture.

My instincts said he was hiding something major in there and I went on a treasure hunt, I found many treasures and was soon happy id come in the room. I found diamonds, Rolex Watches, gold chains, and more diamonds, I could tell it was serious, I even found bullets and my mouth began to water. I was ready to leave, I was about to, but the bullets kept making me want to find their mate, I lifted a lid next to the door exit, thinking a gun could fit in there and I felt like a lottery winner. To this day I don't know If there was a gun in that container, I never looked all I could see was the brand new hundred-dollar bill inside, he could keep his guns I'd buy my own! I had never seen so much money except on TV and it was mine, there were so many hundred-dollar bills that I stopped counting, I got discouraged thinking it would take too long, and thinking maybe I couldn't count that high.

I immediately got nervous, like rich people do when they get around poor people. I started getting all my mother things and my things together, I was packing to leave right now, and she wasn't even there, I was tripping. Then I started looking out the window, waiting for her to get back, she was taking too long! Then I got tired of waiting and left on my own I got around the corner and realized I had no idea where I was going. I needed to hurry back and wait for her to get there.

She finally came back, she was tipsy and laughing with Patty when she came in the room. I shocked her, I was wide awake, fully dressed and all our things were on the bed. My mother knew her son she asked "what did you do" I didn't lie to my mother, I hadn't lied to her since the dynamics of our relationship changed. I dramatically threw a handful of one hundred-dollar bills at her, told her I was hers and we had to go. She was upset, but she didn't allow it to stop her from going through the motions of saving her son.

This man wasn't some old fool, he was something altogether different and my mother knew that, I was just a silly kid who thought life was a get rich adventure without any consequences for the efforts. In truth even in the blue-collar world it wasn't easy to become successful, nor did you get there without making enemies. There was no difference in that regard, the major difference was in the response of the enemies made. In the streets the police don't get involved until after the response, there is no civil court, one person goes to criminal court, while the other goes to the hospital, if they're lucky.

My mother was aware of all those realities and despite the people I'd hurt up until this point, I was naïve to this. I thought I was invincible and the truth is I caught a few breaks, the main one was that Darlene was my mother. She called a cab and we went to a hotel, I bought the best available for all three of us, Patty was one of my moms ride or die so she came with us. The following day we headed to Washington DC in route to Camden New Jersey, the layover in DC was memorable because I convinced my mom to let me buy her a pair of air Jordan's and a CMC sweat suit. This was because all she wore was shoes and never a sweat suit, she was a diva just like my aunt Tilly.

Our Camden destination was because for some reason my mother still thought she could keep me out of Buffalo, and ultimately out of the drug game. So we went to my aunts house in Camden, we were enjoying all our family in Jersey, which are the best. We were spending money like it was raining hundred-dollar bills, I was even pricing thousand-dollar bills at the local bank just to say I had some. When they told me, they cost one thousand one hundred and fifty dollars at the time, and they were only worth the one thousand dollars if I ever wanted to cash them in, I was good, and I didn't need them that bad.

In life all good things must come to an end, one day I seen a car I liked that was for sale and realized id be broke if I purchased it. This woke me up quick and I started shopping for a drug connect, I was ready to finally do what I always dreamed of and start making some serious money. It didn't take long, and my mother was disappointed, but she didn't try to ride my back. There was nowhere on this earth that she could drag me to that I wasn't going to find myself in this life. I may falter but I was always determined in chasing down my self-destruction, this was the only road I knew my way down.

I quickly found two separate drug connections, one for my crack and another one for my marijuana, I was told by some guys that I met through my female cousins that I could make a lot of money with both. Things were going great, I had my signature bags for crack, which fittingly had the skull and crossbones on each bag. I was making money easily, and then karma bit me in the butt.

What goes around comes around, life has taught me this many time over now that I've lived longer. However, at fifteen I didn't know this, so life taught me my first major lessons, I was doing pretty good with the help of my workers, which were guys id met through my cousin. As a reward to them after they begged me, I went out on the town with them. I was never a party person, still not, I wasn't into the entire scene, but they were. So we went out on me, and I was treating them to whatever they wanted. Although I was still a kid, I didn't appear to be, so it was easy to get into the club. They didn't ask for I.D my I.D was that I looked older and I had money. While we were out suddenly, my cousins' boyfriend said he didn't feel good and he left. I had a feeling it was a set up, I felt it was the plan all along, but I was arrogant, and I dismissed the thought in my mind, there was no way these guys would take anything from me, I'd hurt them if they violated.

I'm sure this is probably some the exact thoughts that our family friend had before I took all that I took from him. About an hour later, suddenly everyone was ready to leave and now I really felt something was wrong, I went back to the house and as soon as I got there I asked my cousin where her boyfriend was. She told me he stopped by for a second but then he had to leave. I raced upstairs to the room where I had all my drugs, and found them all gone, then I checked for my money that was locked away in my aunts safe and it was still there.

He only knew the drugs were in that room, nothing else and had he looked around he would've found it. This told me without a doubt no one else did this, it had to be one of the people that knew where to go get what was missing. My thoughts were to kill him and his friends, but then a strange thing happened. I started thinking, and this was a first I was usually a person who only knew how to react and to do so poorly but I suddenly had something to lose. I couldn't recognize he significance of this then, in fact I wasn't even aware of the change.

Prior to that point I was living without a care in the world, I knew

I Confess

what I wanted, and I was recklessly chasing after it void of care of how I got it. I had nothing to lose, I had nothing I cared about even myself, so thinking about my actions or the consequences of them was a foreign concept. Then I became a bit of an overnight success, I was in the exact position I'd fantasized of reaching. This changed my approach, it made my actions matter because now I had something to lose that I placed value on.

I decided to take my time, think of the right way tom respond and do it in a way that wouldn't put myself in a position where I'd lose everything I was building. My words, nor my thought process was this clear, it is only now that I can identify my actions. In the end, after making my efforts to properly respond, I took a trip back home to Buffalo. My goal was to visit my granny love, whom I missed, make a few dollars while there, and purchase a gun I could us to accomplish my plan. While in Buffalo I got up with my shady cousin, he immediately seen I wasn't the same. We were hanging out for a few days and we ended up meeting this family from Chicago that lived across the street from the house my cousin was living in with Angie. We ended up hanging with one of the three sons name Tone G, he was a notorious gang member from the south side of Chicago, which he referred to as the graveyard. I liked him immediately, he looked exactly how you would expect a notorious gang member to, the long hair, charisma and everything.

I was there to have fun, so I decided to treat them to the movies, we went with a few girls, had a great time, and after it was over Tone as well as my cousin agreed to come to Camden with me. This was perfect, now I had a team to return with, it would be smooth and they could just leave town like a thief in the night. When we got back to Camden my aunt knew I brought a new element back with me, and the element was trouble. She talked to me and tried to talk some good sense into me. I love and respect her, so I listened. My shady cousin was always into parties, girls and drinking. He wanted to do all these that night, so I took them to one of the clubs. It was the weekend, so it was very lively that night, and in hindsight this was a huge mistake. My cousin was doing a lot of flirting, while Tone was a lady magnet with his light skin, long hair and uninterested expression. This lead to the local guys feeling a bit jealous, and it soon turned into a fight which lead to something altogether different. My plan was out the window, the only part that came to fruition was they did leave like thieves in the night. The only problem is, it was the same night I was with them. My uncle got us back to Buffalo just as fast as we'd come, and I was told to stay there, my aunt was done with my trouble.

I was back in Buffalo, and it wasn't all a disappointment, but it did change my life dramatically. I wasn't exactly living a Christian life in Jersey, but I was doing a lot better than I would've in Buffalo. My quality of life was about to change in many ways, for one in Jersey in 1993 I didn't need to carry my gun on me every second of the day. In Buffalo I had to carry and use it, Yeah I was back, my mother decided to give it one more chance, and it almost worked, but my fate was sealed.

Confessions of the accused

Chapter 9

Friends with a killer

My first few weeks home, I literally went home. When I left eighty-five Landon when I was twelve years old I vowed to never return. I didn't really feel I was going against my pledge, because I was paying Granny Love money for my room and board. She didn't ask for it, I insisted on it, and took an upstairs room.

I wasn't there much, I was out selling drugs and trying to reestablish myself. I had just lost my entire operation, things were like night and day in comparison. In Jersey things can seem like legit a business, you had to develop certain business skills, such as marketing your product and building your brand. After you did these successfully your business ran itself if you employed the right people, which I hadn't. being back in Buffalo there was no organization at all, it was every man for himself and only the strongest of many would survive. So I was back to being required to operate with an element of violence, or be destroyed by my peers.

I had no desire to lose, I refused, and would barter with my life not to. My mind, or what little of it I had at the time was made up and by all means I intended to reach for the stars, in the hood this isn't as high for us as it is for others. The truth is, some jewelry, a nice car, a couple guns, and five to ten thousand dollars is considered great. This level of achievement is success is many lives are sacrificed for even less, mines happened to be each second that passed I was losing more and more of myself.

I was a bit intrigued by Tone G, his brothers, mother, and sister they seemed to be very much unified, loyal to each other and they had this obvious love for one another. So I started to hang around Titus street with them, and so did my cousin shady. In fact, he was around them much more often. They would go clubbing together, I wasn't into this, so I'd usually end up selling drugs instead of partying with them.

My shady cousin had feuds going on with people from all walks of life do in part to shady dealings, as well as feuds over females. Subsequently these issues caused a few incidents to occur when I wasn't around. One Incident lead to Tone G killing a man who wanted to have a street fight with my cousin. Tone stated where he was from, which was south side Chicago and there was no fighting especially no fair fights. He told my cousin along with his brother to walk away, then told this person to do the same in the other direction as he pulled out his gun. The man took off running up sycamore tone fired one shot and killed the man.

I was told about the incident, and I felt a close connection towards him afterwards. He was cold, calculating and demanded respect of all, any one foolish enough to no give it to him died. There was no middle ground, no compromise and if you were a friend, a brother or family of any kind, then no one dared to cause you any harm without feeling his wrath. I immediately in awe of how he carried himself.

Another night out, my shady cousin ran into one of his lifelong enemies' name CJ, they had been fighting over a female they had both been dealing with for years. When CJ seen my cousin, he planned to kill him that night, and would've done so if it wasn't for Tone being there. This calculated night was no accident, my shady cousin took Tone there hoping they would see CJ so that Tone could kill him. Something my cousin didn't have the heart to do because he feared CJ. The truth was, CJ was a notorious shooter who had no hang ups with killing, and this scared my cousin. This is until he met someone more ruthless, much more capable and willing to kill. There was simply no match between the two. Tone was born into one of those most notorious gangs, the gangster disciples, raised in one of the most notorious neighborhoods, and in the midst of it all he became one the most notorious of his era.

So that night when shady took him to the castle point he did so knowing there was a great chance he'd see CJ, and Tone had proven to him weeks earlier that kill anyone who tried to cause him the least bit of harm. The bad thing is, shady didn't tell tone, nor anyone else of the feud or the dangers of going to a place where CJ would likely be since it was in his neighborhood and it was the place to be on a Friday night in 1993.

When CJ arrived, he noticed shady, he approached and there was immediately an exchange of gunfire inside the club that had virtually no security. As a result, neither shooter was hit, CJ or Tone. The shooters got away and the feud was no longer between Shady and CJ, it was now between two strangers of one another.

It was in the midst of this that I started hanging out almost exclusively on Titus with Tone and his family. However after the shooting at the club, shady started avoiding Tone and Tone noticed. This started to cause friction because it was obvious that now that shady started this feud he no longer wanted anything to do with it. Tone was literally hunting CJ at all hours of the day, but CJ wasn't just sitting around, he was returning the favor. So there were shoot outs, thing were escalating and even Tone's mother got in between an incident one morning when CJ and his right hand man b-boy came looking for Tone on pedal bikes.

With all this going on, shady was across the street, basically hiding in the house, pretending he was sick, or that his girlfriend wouldn't let him leave out the house. This eventually infuriated Tone, and one day he told Shady how he felt as well as his repercussions, Tone said " I killed for you, and I'm in these streets everyday fighting a beef that isn't mines because I like you, but before I let some female come between the bond we got, I'll go in that and blow her brains out".

He had a way with words, as well as the tone in his voice that made you believe him, and not question the authenticity of them. His words scared my cousin because he knew he'd bitten off more than he could chew. He promised Tone he would get up with him later and convinced him all was well. Then he instead went to some other guys in the area and told them some lie about Tone wanting to move on them and told them he could help set Tone up for them to get him first.

By this time Tone had a reputation, he was deadly, and truth is Buffalo wasn't ready or a mentality like his. He was very shocking to the spirits of men that in that environment was deemed notorious. To him, and what they were used to in Chicago they were elementary, and out of fear they planned to kill Tone with the help of Shady. They didn't know everything he told them was a lie, and he had his own reasons to want Tone out the way which was to save his own life.

A few days passed, shady came around much more, but unknown to us it was only to be close enough to tone to set him up. It took him about a week, and Tone had come down with some kind of flu bug that knocked him off his feet. He decided that while he was sick he'd stay at his girlfriends' house where only his most trusted family and friends would know about. This was shady's opportunity, he called these men and took them to where Tone was. However, they decided to make sure shady couldn't tell by having him participate in the shooting.

They approached the front window, they could see through the sheer curtains, they saw tone laying on the front couch. They shot through the window, both shady and one of the other two assailants, while the third waited in the gold Lincoln. Tone could've retreated further to the back of the house and saved his life; however he was raised to be a G, it wasn't just his name, it was how he lived. He had a gun beside the couch, as he was being shot he retrieved the weapon and tried to approach the gunfire returning fire. The heavy pellets coming from both weapons, one a person he called a friend, was simply too much, and the bullets consumed him.

My cousin shady called me after this shooting, he confided in me about it, as well as his reasoning. He was cared, Tone had him living in fear, and its hard he did what he'd done to save his life. He cried his drunken confession, and his words ripped, then tore at the strings of my heart. I didn't know Tone long, but in the few months I knew him he proved to be a friend. In the hood its hard to meet people you can trust, people you can count on to always be real, and not stab you in the back no matter what. Tone was all this and more, I knew without any doubt he'd never be anything but a true friend, he'd never turn, never tell, and with most you could only hope, but with him you knew he was a true friend and a true G. I got his name on my right forearm, and I mourn him as a brother.

My relationship with shady was never the same, it was strange at best, I loved him like an older brother, the absolute truth was that I looked up to him since I was a little boy. This confused my young heart tremendously because I was at odds with my feelings about him, and the man he was responsible for killing. I was so confused as to where my loyalty should be that I didn't even attend the funeral of my friend, and even shady sick, twisted self, went like he was Tupac in juice and I think he got a kick out of it. I started to focus on my hustle, avoiding shady as much as possible, I wasn't scared I just couldn't trust him. I loved him, he was my big cousin, but even more than that he was a friend. However, I was having trouble trying to process what he'd done so I started to deal with him in small doses. I eventually did my best to push it to the back of my mind, holding on to it as a point of reference regarding his character.

Then about two months later, give or take a few weeks, shady was arrested, and as his family, as well as friend I held him down. Anything he needed, between me and his girlfriend Angie it was taken care of. Sadly, this good deed wouldn't go unpunished for either of us.

Shady had a child on the way by another girl, between helping him personally, helping Angie to raise his lawyer money, I was also helping his child to be. At fifteen this was a lot, and I still had my own life to manage as best as I could. Things were very stressful, but I didn't complain, I did as any true friend should, I held it down.

Despite the feeling I had lying dormant about his involvement in the murder of Tone, I went hard for shady. It was Angie and I, we did whatever to make the money his lawyer needed. The two of us bonded in the following days, and months. It was unknown to us that people had started creating rumors that the two of us bonded in the following days, and months. We were completely unaware of the rumors, we were too focused on doing whatever we needed to in order to get Shady home. At the same time someone was telling shady that the two of us were involved with each other sexually, and he decided to keep it to himself instead of telling either of us.

After we reached our goal, his lawyer had his money and shady we saved from many years in state prison, we fell back from each other. There was never any sex between us, not even a kiss, the fact is the two of us were so focused on doing what we could to hustle up the money for shady that sex want on either of our minds, not with each other or anyone else. Hindsight says, shady was simply unable to identify what loyalty looked like because he had none of the identifying qualities in himself.

Once this was done I was also broke and miserable because I was all out of options to get back on my feet. My mentor from my youth and I had been off and on, more off than on. So my pride was keeping me from going to him plus shady had went to jail with some unfinished business between them, and I felt guilty by association. In truth, had I gone to him he would've happily helped me out, but I didn't, in fact I avoided him.

Out of desperation I eventually did one of my own grease bucket moves. It was something I had done a few times in the past to get out of a hole, so I was familiar with my own version of being shady. I would take twenty dollars, as I did this day, and go to Doris Records to purchase a jar of comeback. This was usually used as a form of cut for drugs. However, having no drugs to cut, id simply cook the comeback with baking soda as if it was crack. I'd usually do it with a few people, then I'd buy real drugs by the time they realized the comeback was void of the main ingredient. Then when they'd come back to complain, I'd replace the "mistake" with the real crack. My customers would then see me as a very trustworthy person, and they'd look to do all their business with me.

It was a long way from where I'd been several months earlier, and I was depressed. I would think of Jersey a lot, and I'd often reminisce about my friend Tone. I had reached my lowest point, and I started to regret many things. As I reflect, I know that I was clinically depressed the whole time, and I was simply avoiding dealing with the real source of my depression. I had a classic case of a victim blocking out trauma in order to survive.

Unfortunately in the hood, where people are trained to always be okay, 'even when you're not' I didn't stand a chance of being noticed, or my issues being diagnosed. I was on my own, sadly this meant I was headed to much worse days. There was simply no other options available, and this remains true to so many black and brown boys in the hood.

Confessions of the accused

Chapter 10

Running out of time

Since my return to buffalo it had been one misstep after another. I simply couldn't get my feet settled up under me, and I was constantly on edge, fighting for every inch in life. Barely making it, and completely uncertain, an opportunity for change was presented to me by an unlikely source.

I would often go to my Granny Love's house at certain times to accept collect calls from Shady on a separate phone line I had set up for him. I would make three-way calls, and talk to him about countless things, this is how my opportunity for change came to me, shady met some girls that lived in Bradford Pennsylvania, and he told me I should go out there, and see how it was. He told me he was locked up with someone who said it was nice out there. I told him I'd think about it, and then he revealed his own reason behind bringing it up. The girls wanted to see him and another guy, they were coming to Buffalo, he wanted me to make sure they got to the county jail in Wende. I helped with the visit, and soon after he started telling me I should go check out Bradford, I wasn't really doing much, I was virtually going in circles and I was all over the place but had no real stability so I agreed. These two girls come to Buffalo to pick me up one night, and without hesitation I jumped in the caravan in search of a fresh start.

I went there the pretense that id find a situation like Jersey waiting for me. The truth was, that was all I had on my mind, I had finally had a little taste of a minor portion of success and only for a split second, I wanted it back. I was shocked when on the ride back Tisha, 'one of females that was supposedly my cousin Shadys girl came on to me in the van while Reeba drove. My mind wasn't on sex at all, and now I think of it my mind hadn't been on sex since I first got my hands on the money in Richmond Virginia.

I didn't reject Tisha, she was attractive, voluptuous woman. I simply had absolutely no interest in anything other than regaining my lost ground. So as we rode and she continued to try her best to physically please me, I went along with it. However my mind was preoccupied, I was in a state of depression that had gone unrecognized, and I was obsessed with using money to medicate my deep rooted pain.

We arrived in Bradford, it was after midnight so there wasn't much to see, I couldn't tell if it was a huge city, or in the middle of some country style town. I fixed my clothes, Tisha felt insecure thinking that she couldn't please me because I failed to have an orgasm. I had no way of telling her the truth, I didn't even know what it was. In fact, I didn't even realize I didn't ejaculate, my mind was completely removed from any sexual pleasures.

I was met by a lively house full of people, they were drinking, and carrying on. I was the only black face in the house, everybody else was white, with the exception of Tisha and Reeba's housemate Tammy's boyfriend, and he was Mexican. I was instantly comfortable, I didn't feel judged or on the defense, they didn't appear to see me as a threat which was what I was used to around people that look just like me. I mean I've been over my own family members house and got the judgmental and defensive look, so this was more comforting as well as different.

Things were cool, they offered me drinks and the usual party favors, I declined informing them and I didn't change. I was pretty drained, my emotions were raw from anticipation of the unknown, and the ride, Tisha noticed and took me to the bedroom to sleep. She had other ideas, she was probably curious to see if it was something wrong with her, or if it was me, so she was all over me, and I turned into an animal. I took my frustrations out on her body, and she concluded it wasn't it, it was that I didn't like what she did to me in the van. All of her thoughts were off base, I loved sex, especially oral sex, which is what had taken place in the van. The truth was more complex and multi layered, I wouldn't even recognize what it was for many years, so for her to just guess it correctly would be almost impossible.

Days passed on, things were slow, the town was pretty small and quiet compared to anywhere id ever lived, but I actually liked it. Tisha and I became a couple without many words, it just happened. I just went with the flow, as I continued to search for my opportunity to reach towards my goals. I was obsessed with being able to deal drugs and use money as my pain reliever.

The opportunity came when I was on the brink of giving up and leaving Bradford, this drug addict that lived around the corner came over, I was warned not to deal with her, and told she was a crack head. Unknown to my Warner, she was the very person id been daydreaming of since my arrival, in fact before I ever got in the van to come here! I discreetly found out where she lived, then I snuck over there, and we had a conversation.

I told her I could anything, I asked her what would be the best thing to get. I asked her how things are done, what's the prices paid, I treated her like she was my college professor. I needed all her answers in order to ace my final exams. She was a well of information that I needed, she told me how to win without even knowing it. In her mind she was running game, to her I was the new fool she was going to use. Unfortunately she was unaware of who my mother was, she had no way of knowing that these kids eyes, with the curious look in them had been

I Confess

born to a woman who prepared me for her kind long before I could spell the word game.

I left, and I was ready to execute my mission. The thing is, I was broke, and home wasn't around the corner. I was about an hour and a half outside of my hometown, with zero resources. I was eating and living off Tisha, which made me feel like a sucka every second of everyday. I had to get back home, I had to do it with a sure plan to make a move, and return with some product.

After a few days it developed, I would get the money from Tisha and contact my mentor. I hadn't been around cold spring in a long time, my name wasn't out in the streets with trouble maker attached to it. I made some calls and set up my trip to go visit my family, and we went. It was Tisha, Reeba, and I, on the road to see the family. As soon as I arrived, family was the last thing on my mind, I went to my Granny Loves house, I seen my family, but I was there to make a call to my mentor.

I met up with him, told him what I had been up to, and that id fell off, and I told him why. He told me the reason I was having problems, and he was right. I was trying to do too much, and be too many things at once. It wasn't enough for me to get money, I needed all the extra stuff. I needed to be seen, needed to be known, needed people to fear me, love me, and respect me.

These goals conflict with each other, and they especially ran into a conflict with being successful in a game where many of my goals were a hindrance to becoming very successful. He reminded me of a day when he tried to get me to find someone to do a job for him, asked me did I remember, I did remember. My mentor came to me, told me a guy owed him a lot of money and was playing games. He told me the guy had just purchased a new pearl white Mercedes Benz, it was at the dudes' mothers house, and hadn't yet been insured. He told me to have one of my boys firebomb the car, and he'd pay them four ounces of cocaine, or ten thousand dollars cash. I told my mentor "forget that I'll do it myself, you can give it to me"! he was upset and disappointed he told me " I'm trying to teach you how to be a boss, how to get things done without being on the front line, the dudes on the front line go to jail, or die early and broke, I'm trying to teach you how to do this right but you keep wanting to be the fool, never mind forget I asked you about this".

I did remember, I had never forgot and since that day our relationship had been stained. He embarrassed me, and I didn't know how to tell him that I had been damaged. I didn't know how to tell him I felt like all I deserved was being used. I didn't know how to tell him this because I really didn't know this. I believed I felt opposite, yet I lived through my actions as if all I was worth was an early death, or a prison cell.

He made his point, told me I didn't need to give him the short money I had, told me to keep it, and stop by the house to see him later, I agreed, knowing I was supposed to be in Buffalo quickly as I'd told Tisha and Reeba. However, there was no way I would leave here empty handed, and there was no way I'd leave without going to see my mentor.

I told Tisha an Reeba, they agreed to hang out and wait for me. That night, at about 8pm I went by his house, we spoke, and he told me I could take anything I wanted (as far as quantity of drugs) back to Bradford with me. He simply wanted me to be smart and stop playing both sides of the game. I really didn't think I'd need that much drugs because Bradford was small, very small and a ten-dollar bag of crack in Buffalo was worth fifty dollars in Bradford. I did the math, and decided to take a quarter ounce of cocaine that I'd cook up myself. It was worth more than three thousand where I was going, and I knew I'd have to go slow, or end up in custody of the police.

Things got good for me quick, and before long I was back in Buffalo, I was back and forth a lot because I was also selling marijuana through a few people I had dealing for me. The marijuana would be gone in no time, and I was frequently coming home. Things were good, and even Shamel had come back to Buffalo, so I'd come to spend time with my brother from another mother. I even tried to convince him to come stay in Bradford, he lasted there a week before he was homesick and ready to go.

Then one day while I was in Buffalo my cousin Tim asked me to come. I was long past any surface feelings of what he'd done to me as a little boy, I had done my best to actually make it my fault, and simply view it as childhood experimentation on my part. I refused to view it as being victimized because by this time I wasn't a little boy, had I allowed myself to view it as sexual assault that had traumatized me I would've killed him. So I took the blame from him, then placed it and the shame onto myself. This allowed me to protect the secret because it was something I'd been wrong to do, so I had to hide it. It was a classic case of victim's shame, and I couldn't even spell victim, let alone be able to identify myself as having been.

So when he wanted to come to Bradford I quickly agreed, never thinking of how creepy I used to feel around him. Then these feelings started to come right back when he'd be around me in Bradford, especially if there was any threat of us being alone. I would avoid that at all costs as much as I possibly could, and the excuses for it in my head were complex, I didn't know how to articulate them, so I mostly ignored as I avoided him.

Then soon after it was apparent that he planned to stay and he was going to be living with all of us, it was time for me to do my best to relocate. It wouldn't be easy, the town was small and I didn't know many people. My only real connections were Tisha and Reeba, outside of them the rest were business. There were a few females but nothing really stable.

One day without warning, two people that id heard of, but never seen came by the house. It was a white girl, blonde hair, blue eyes, she was about 5'6 145lbs her name was Jennifer, and the little midnight black man was about 5'3, noticeably shorter than her, his name was little Dave. I could immediately tell they were a much different element than I was used to in Bradford, which got my attention. I'd been told that Jennifer was his prostitute, and that he sends her to Canada to turn tricks for him, I was intrigued, and wanted to know if he did this because he got high, but he doesn't anymore. I had heard that before but I had to see it for myself.

The two soon moved into a studio apartment right on main street in Bradford. This was actually the main place of attraction in this small town. On the weekends the young teenagers and adults would go to Main Street to hang out. Those who had cars would drive back and forth down Main Street. They called this "flaming the main". People would really flame the main until the wee hours of the morning playing music, while others would be on foot doing the same. This was where all the excitement took place, and now Jennifer and little Dave lived right on the strip.

I started to hang over there often, hanging with Lil Dave. Jennifer also has three of her four kids living with them, Nathan, Tony, and Abigail. I preferred being over there to being in that house because it started to feel weird. I couldn't quite put my finger on it at the time, I simply liked not being there. I soon started doing my drug business over there on main and my customers grew. Lil Dave knew people, and he started to make me money through other sources. I would pay him to move some of my drugs for me, along with a few other people. Things were starting to pick up, I started to deal with people from surrounding towns. I even started to cross back over state lines, going into Olean NY, dealing with guys that sold drugs out this bar called "the pub".

Then one day I had to meet with someone in the New York state side of business, I told Lil Dave to ride with me, he really did not want to go, because he had a NYS warrant. I talked him into riding, and subsequently we got pulled over for no apparent reason. The police seemed to only want one thing, they ran a warrant check, and just as they expected Lil Dave had a warrant. They took him into custody, they let me and my driver, a Dominican buddy of mines go. That arrest was always suspicious to me, and It took me years before I was able to conclude that someone had called the cops on Lil Dave.

I did all I could to bail him out, it was impossible, so I made sure he had everything he needed while in custody. I took Jennifer to see him, even went in with her once, even though I didn't want to go in no one's prison. I felt it was my fault, so I went to see him, not realizing this was the same reality I was spending night, and day chasing down. I was moving way too fast to notice signs all on the walls around me. There would be plenty of time to read them later, right then, I had to get that money, it was all that mattered, no price was too high to pay for it.

Some weeks later, business is smooth, life is great, and only getting better so when Jennifer told me to go to a party with her I did. Her friend , and friends boyfriend were having a party. I really didn't want to deal with her friends boyfriend, and he would always screw his face up around as if he was mad there was another black guy around. He felt the only black guy around should be him, at least this is how it seemed to me. I had no idea that two of the females I was involved with sexually were females that he would sleep with behind his girlfriend's back. I didn't know what his issue was at that time, and I didn't care so I went. Plus I was still staying with Jennifer after her man went to jail, she didn't even want my money, I felt the least I could do is go to a party with her.

We were all dancing, It was in a small apartment, crowded as a can of sardines. I didn't know anyone, so I danced with Jennifer, I wasn't going to have anyone else dancing on my man's girl. I can't even lie, I didn't know how to dance, and this wasn't my scene at all. Whenever I've gone to a party, or club prior to this I was always holding up a wall. I was never comfortable enough to be dancing, a girl could come dance in front of me, but that's about it. I didn't even care that night, Jennifer talked me right into just having fun which I did

Then she took me to the back in the kitchen, she told me to try her drink. I told her you know I don't drink, she said " me either, this isn't liquor it is a wine cooler, just taste It it's not what you think". I tasted her wine cooler, it tasted like a peach drink not alcohol, but I didn't allow myself to drink but a little of it. We danced some more, and somewhere between sips of the wine cooler, and dancing there was kissing. My head was spinning, I wasn't drunk, I was buzzed, but I was also feeling a bit of betrayal in my bones. This couldn't be right, in fact it wasn't, but I didn't stop.

We went home and had the wildest sex all night long, we were out of our heads, having an out of body experience, when it was over, and there was no turning back. The next few weeks things continued, she even went to go see Lil Dave with me encouraging her, and even took a trip to Canada to make her money the way she knew how with me discouraging her. I told her she didn't have to, but she didn't want to just sit around, she wanted to pull her own weight for her and her kids. We tried to keep that status quo, big things were escalating between us.

I can remember when I started to realize both of us were starting to get serious. I brought a few of my duded to the town from Buffalo, I had met my boy Terrell through my cousin Shady, while they were in lock up together. I would make three way calls for Terrell, then when he came home I tried to put him on his feet. I had him with me in Bradford and a bunch of girls over the house. We were having fun and this one Spanish girl was a bit drunk, she was really freaky. When Terrells cousin was in the room, having sex with her, I went inside and Jennifer was hot on my tail a few minutes later. She was flipping like we were married, and I was hiding what I was doing with other females.

It had been weeks since we'd taken the trip to see Lil Dave, and I had stopped trying to talk her into going. Our one-night indiscretion had become a relationship, and there was no more trips to Canada either. My birthday had come upon us, when we realized we had the same birthday. She was turning twenty-four, and unknown to her I was turning sixteen. We started to settle in, and it seemed natural, like it was meant to be.

Every time, without fail, when life started to get stable for me somethings would go wrong. I was doing great, money was good, I was even in love, or as close as I was going to get to it at sixteen. I had settled in and there were no signs that trouble was lurking. Then it came knocking, and it sent our lives into a whirlwind.

The first customer I ever had in Bradford had gotten busted, she didn't know that I knew about it, but I knew everything in that town. She was busted across state lines, to buy crack. I had strict rules, which is why even the police respected me in Bradford at the time. There was order, I ran things like a business, and there were no complaints against me. All traffic to our door stopped by 12am. The bar below us closed at 2am as well as the one across the street. So before traffic robbed me of my camouflage, I was already shut down. This upset some, but most understood.

I simply had no control of the few like this fool, and she got busted in the middle of the night, going to buy at the pub in Olean. She told me, made a deal, and was released, in order to trap me with a sell. I was two years ahead of her and her games. Like I said, I was born to the right person that had taught me how to survive. When she came, she had way too much money, she never had this kind of money. This along with the fact she was out of jail was enough to warn me not to deal with her, so I didn't.

The problem was, she already had the heat on me, and my residence. I had to figure out a way to buy time, so I told her an elaborate lie. Told her my drug connect had cut me off, told me I was too hot " I was speaking directly into the wire she was wearing". I told her to let me get dressed, see if I could go talk to him, and get him to deal with her directly. Then I had her follow me half way, then told her to wait, allowing her to see me to go this guys house, same house the party was at that Jen and I first kissed. I came back, told her he would not deal with her, and I stopped by to talk to him for a few about something then left.

She begged me to please get her something from him, anything at all. I took the money, went in the hallway at his house, pretended to buy from him, and the left. I gave her what her, and the police thought was from him.

I had to shut down my operation after this, there was a police car stationed outside our apartment, and Jennifer took her innocent looking self out there to ask what the issue was. She was told, there was a reported drug trafficking coming from the apartment. They were told to watch the apartment until the state police could serve a search warrant on the place. We had taken what we could, and we were in the U-HAUL on our way to Buffalo by the next day. When the warrant was served, it was served on both places, the one I'd lead the girl, as well as the one I'd fled.

Confessions of the accused

Chapter 11

You can run but you can't hide

Back in Buffalo, this time I'm not alone. I got a ready-made family, a twenty-four year old woman and her three kids. Their ages were eight, five and two years old. My luck was holding so far because my mother had a nice two bedroom apartment she had recently rented which she was trying to use as an incentive for me to come back to Buffalo.

So when I found myself in need of a place and let her know the situation she did as she had always done, she came through for her son. She was hardly there, the place was newly renovated and my mother hadn't really made it a home yet. She cleared her personal things out of the house and we moved in. We put the boys together with their bunk beds in one room and two year old Abigail had her bed in the master bedroom with us. We managed to make the abrupt transition a smooth one for the kids which was important. This move wasn't cheap and when the dust settled money was low. The bills were soon coming and there was no income. I was beyond stressed, there was simply no way a kid my age could handle this pressure without breaking but I was determined not to break.

After getting up with my mentor who was upset I returned to Buffalo, he told me to take my time and get myself together. He didn't want me to return to Cold Spring at all and I really didn't think it was best either.

So I had to figure things out and he was done holding my hand a long time ago so it was my problem to sort out.

Jennifer came up with a bright idea that I didn't want to agree to and I regret I gave in. She asked me if I wanted her to go to Canada for the weekend, she could easily make anywhere from fifteen to eighteen hundred over a short weekend. This would take care of the bills and give me some room to put my hustle together.

This is when things started to fall apart, first she took this other girl with her named Becky that I used to mess around with but had stopped and she remained our friend. She had no experience at all and never should have been with her. It wasn't long before things went wrong. The same night both were arrested and since Jennifer was known she was held, Becky was sent across the border.

Now not only was I broke, my woman was in jail and I had three kids to take care of with no idea of how long. There was simply no way I was going to turn my back on Jennifer or the kids so I had to figure out how to gain control of the situation.

It was here that I learned firsthand what single parents go through. I'll forever respect the single parents that roll their sleeves up and put the needs of their children ahead of their own. I didn't do the job justice, I did my best though.

The streets weren't an option, I had these kids. I had to cook for them, clean for them and make sure Abigail hair was done. I had no time to leave to hustle and risk them losing both of us. So I struggled instead and thank God Ma Duke, Shamel's mother would come get Abigail almost every day. She sometimes wouldn't even bring her back to me. I missed my little lady but I was relieved at the same time and I'm sure parents know what I mean.

I can't pretend to be a saint, I was doing as best as I could as Jennifer and I waited for the Queen to return as they say to their detainee's in Canada. I was taking her collect calls and I was making my best efforts.

However I was still a immature kid and I made poor choices that lead to many levels of betrayal.

One of them was when I invited a girl I had met about a year prior over to the house. The kids were gone, Ma Duke had Abby as always and the boys were at my Granny love's house with my mother. I wasn't really getting to see her much since we had met, Nicole had strict parents and I wasn't really in Buffalo much. So this small window of opportunity opened for us and we both ran through it like the hot blooded teenagers we were. We had a quickie that probably lasted two minutes and from that we produced my daughter De'aria.

Soon after this encounter I decided at about day fifteen that I needed some help. I was getting a bit overwhelmed and I was running out of things I knew how to cook. So after a few days and the Queen still hadn't returned I went to one of my old flings I had that I knew was a good person. I basically kidnapped her off her doorstep in her socks and brought her to the house and she stayed over for about eight days to help out. It was beyond wrong and I have no excuse. I did my best with what I had but I didn't have much at that time.

I gave it my all, I put all the arrogance and pride I had aside. I even took my expensive stereo system and pawned it so that the kids could eat. I was hanging on by a thread and honestly don't know how I managed. I can only give praise to God for sending the helpers that were sent my way.

Jennifer got out after about thirty days and it was one of the happiest days of my life. I knew then that I would never put her at risk where she would lose her freedom and those kids be taken from their mother. I came close to breaking this promise I had made to myself but thank God I escaped breaking it. God knows it was only one of the few I was able to actually keep.

Things were rocky when she got home and it was because I had done a poor job of hiding my infidelity. The kids never saw a lot or anything inappropriate in the way of physical contact. However they seen more than they should have and Jennifer was rightfully upset.

We patched things up and in the mean time I was still broke and starting to feel worthless. It would soon be September and time to put the boys in school. Something had to give, something had to happen fast.

One night my brother Shamel and my childhood friend Lil Jason were at the house. They were smoking marijuana and I decided to try some. It was a big mistake, I was high and I told them let's go get some more of that. We got in a cab to go to the drug house they got it from. I came on the porch, they didn't even know my plan, I was tripping off whatever they had let me smoke.

When the female opened the door to give them the marijuana they asked for, I pulled out my gun, I forced everyone into the house. I told them to give me everything. I was high but not too high to notice that one of the females was pregnant. She was about seven months and was in the house selling drugs. I thought she had to be out of her mind but who the hell was I to judge her? I had to be at least just as crazy as she was. Here I was forcing my way into a house that was pitch black except for the light coming from the television. There could have been someone inside waiting to blow my brains out, I didn't know this house or the people inside. I had a death wish, I didn't realize it until I was literally chasing it up and down the streets of Buffalo.

We left there with a box of marijuana and money. I now had the munchies as they say, so I had the cab take us to geraldine's pizza parlor. I ordered me some pizza and other things. I went to wait outside as I seen something that caught my eye. There was a yellow Cadillac outside with a older man and a young girl inside. It was about one in the morning, I knew what that was and seen a opportunity. I approached the car and robbed him too, I was tripping but I didn't care. The drug had given me a excuse to release all my pint up rage and frustration. After the car left speeding away my brother and Lil Jay were ready to leave. I told them I had to get my food and I took my gun back out to go get my food free of charge with a tip.

After that night was over I never smoked again, Jennifer told me I flipped on Shamel and Lil Jason when we got home. She told me whatever I had she don't like me like that. She couldn't believe it was marijuana and as I reflect I know it wasn't. The drug was a excuse, I was on life, nothing has ever made me more out of my mind or got me higher than life itself and I was at my limit.

I came home one day and Jennifer was gone, the kids and all their things were gone. She had left me without word or warning. I guess you can call it self-preservation. Together we were drowning and I was the dead weight taking us under. She had to save herself as well as the children.

Strangely it also gave me the ability to get my feet back up under me solidly. Not that I made no efforts to find her first, I did, but the person that she got to help her refused to betray her trust. She batted her eyes a few times at our neighbor, a old ugly white guy, and he came to the aide of the damsel in distress. Unknown to me he had been helping her to find her own place.

I started to hustle with my cousin Snapper and his right hand man Monet. I came around when things were real shaky and unpredictable. Monet had just accidently shot this woman in her groin area and she had hemorrhaged to death. It was over a petty argument that got out of hand. He was constantly paranoid and didn't trust anyone at that time from that immediate circle. He felt it was a matter of time before someone told it all and he was put in prison. I did my best to calm him and to help him dispose of the weapon he needed to get rid of.

We took a road trip to my old stomping grounds in Bradford and used it as a opportunity to get rid of the weapon. We stayed in Bradford at a hotel for a few days and he got to see the layout of Bradford, but we went back to Buffalo. We had a nice situation already and it simply needed some order. I knew how to bring order, you either did it through finesse or by force and I knew that since it was already too unorganized that I would need to use force.

Sadly I had forgotten all the wise words my mentor had told me and I ran full speed into a operation playing the front line. I was the Johnny come lately of the crew, Snapper and Mo had already been there and everyone was used to the way things had been. They had no desire for change, no interest in structure and consequences for violations or unpaid debts. I instantly became the bad gut and contrary to what they might have thought, I liked it. I fed off of it and knew that I must have been doing things something right.

There were countless very calculating things I did to make everyone think I was crazy. I was far from it, I was a monster at manipulating my audience. I made them believe that I would kill over a dollar, literally one dollar, four quarters, ten dimes, twenty nickels. However you choose to see it, I made them believe I would take their life for it and to prove that their fears were correct, I was prepared to do it. This madness is what gave me a edge and it is also what enabled my inevitable downfall. My mastery of my audience eventually became my undoing and somewhere along the way I got lost in my self-created character. I've since learned that when two exist in a single space with conflicting views someone always has to die so the other may live.

As I got completely lost in the beast at last I found that I had no limits and I knew with no doubts that only death could tame me. I began to cry for death to overtake me, not with actual tears, I had long ago learned not to waste physical energy on tears. Instead I would build and destroy relationships. I would terrorize people on a whim and often void of any provocation. Like a vampire I fed off the blood and misery of others. My daily routine was to build financial riches, however to pass time as well as a method to quell my deep rooted pain, I inflicted many forms of pain onto others. It could have been as simple as being insensitive to a female at the right moment, knowing she cared for me. Or it could have been robbing a garage full of people at a illegal chop shop, knowing they couldn't call the police. I was so out of it and screaming for death daring anyone including God to put me out my misery. The louder I screamed the more it seemed no one could hear me, so I grew bolder. In my own way I had become god like, at least in my madness I felt I had. People feared me just as the most high, no one stopped me, or seemed to be able to. At least not the people I yearned to have do so which were the two who loved me most.

This was the thing, I was running in essence though I was playing the role of a street thug, I was running, which means by definition I was a coward. I wasn't a tough guy at all, but I had to assume the role in order to avoid my truth. The truth was too much to face, it became easier hide and play my character instead. There was simply no other option for me, I would have been unable to cope with my demons, I didn't have the tools to. Had I took off the mask for a second I probably would have killed myself, but no matter how loud I screamed kill me, I wanted to live!

One night I was walking, I was unsure of where I was headed, I was just walking with no real destination. I ran into my boy Terrell, I had not seen him in a while. Last time I had seen him I had called him because of a beef with some drunk guys. It just so happened that when I was about to pull the trigger to shoot one of them point blank in the face, Terrell noticed the police. They had actually hid to watch the incident unfold, then arrest us, him seeing the police saved that drunk boys life and me from going to prison that night.

We sat talking for a minute on Bissell and he asked me was I headed to Jennifer house. I said, no why you say that, he told me he seen her moving around the corner a while back. He told me a old fat white dude had moved her things in with her. I knew he wasn't mistaken, he told me he had been there and had tried to have sex with her but she had backed out on him at the last second. That sounded like my scandalous Jennifer alright, he gave me the layout and address so I could see for myself. I thanked him told him I would get with him at a later date and went to Jennifer's house.

She wasn't home the house was pitch black and I broke in the house to be sure. I guess she hadn't got the lights put on yet but it was her house. I found all these things even letters to her ex in prison telling him all she had been through with me. She had written me as well, I guess she was purging herself. Whatever she was doing she had a serious surprise waiting for her when she got home.

It took a few days, I was coming by periodically throughout the day and night. I had me a new place to go when I needed it. I was making myself at home as if we were back together and in my mind we were after I cursed her sneaky butt out. When she finally came home she could tell she had been found but she didn't leave she waited on me to come. We talked, she made her case and I made mines, and we moved on. We loved each other, yes it was dysfunctional and it was built in part on lies. She found out my real age, she started to see I wasn't the nice guy she thought I was. I had more edge and a lot more darkness than she had ever experienced. This was saying a lot since her last two relationships were with pimps.

Things went back to normal between us despite all the warning signs that we were like a nuclear weapon when mixed. Then things quickly turned ugly because I wasn't the same guy she had left. I was a very different animal all together. My hustle was one thousand times worse than it was in Bradford or while we lived together when we moved to Buffalo. I was completely obsessed and zombified. I would be gone days and she was used to me coming home to eat dinner, she was use to me having structure and discipline to my hustle. The strange thing is I was trying to put those things into place but I wouldn't let them be. I was constantly there not trusting the process at all. I was also doing other things such as robbing drug dealers and anyone else I caught slipping. I had no boundaries, no one was off limits and all my wires were crossed. I would help my partners get on their feet and then rob them only to help them again. It was sick, no I was sick.

So one day I stopped by the house to drop some money off. I didn't fully trust Jennifer again yet due to her running off once. So I was hiding money in the house in different spots. Hiding drugs in the attic before she even knew I knew she lived there. I was about to leave back out and she was supposed to be going to do laundry. She started beefing with me, wanted to know who that was in the car, it was a white fairly attractive woman. I didn't really notice or like her like that.

This white girl was actually the owner of the white Z-24 I was driving. She was a customer, I would often have her car and was trying to buy it. I tried to explain to her that it was business but she didn't believe me and told me if I left not to come back. She told me to take all my stuff now. I thought I was God, I told her, "I don't have enough room to take everything that's mines, everything in here belongs to me including your ass, now shut up I'll be back later".

I should have listened to her crazy butt because she burned the house down! Ours and the people's downstairs, with all my money, drugs, clothes and everything. She took her clothes with the kids to the laundry mat and burned it down. She had the help of one of my close family members. She told her how to make it look like a accident and she did it. The investigation still ruled it suspicious and made her agree to take a lie detector test to be scheduled for a later date.

I was tight, I knew in my gut she had done it on purpose but she was able to convince the fire department and me to give her the benefit of doubt. I had no choice my things were gone and there was no way to claim them in damages. I took a loss I didn't even know the full value of, all I knew was the streets would now have to pay more. I past the streets the bill just like stores do when uncle sam raised the taxes. I wasn't as patient as I used to be, I refused to ever starve while others ate steak. In my mind you had to eat to live, if you didn't eat you died and if I had to die I wasn't dying alone. So I fed on the prey of those that were doing better than me.

After a few weeks of staying in a hotel we found a house on the west side. I refused to let Jennifer associate with my cousin Tony that had influenced her behaviors. I didn't care what she told me and I felt I was right about her doing that house fire so the relationship was done. I had worked extra hard in the streets so I had the money we needed to buy new furniture and appliances. I can't lie, I even knocked my own man for his stash. Monet had left about three thousand dollars worth of crack in the glove box of his car, then went somewhere and I needed that. I was up against the wall at the time, money was okay but I was a animal feeding on every creature in the jungle, even my own kind.

I had gotten lost in my character and it was so intoxicating that I became a fiend. There was no rehab on earth that I could check in for the addiction I had. Drug addicts describe their addictions by using the metaphor of there being a monkey on their back. Well if I was to take a page out their book I would have to say I had three silver back gorillas on my back and each was pulling me in different ways with different agendas.

I did eventually learn months later that my cousin did help Jennifer burn down our apartment. The amazing part is she had convinced me otherwise when she passed the lie detector test issued by the investigators of the fire. I never would have knew but I intercepted a letter my cousin had sent Jennifer which mentioned what they had done. It actually appealed to my sick thinking, I could use this in the future to my advantage.

Confessions of the accused

Chapter 12

The truth shall set you free

My addiction which was hiding me from my pain took me to some of the earth's darkest alley's and inspired some of the worse kinds of evil to form then manifest on my limbs. Money was just away to purchase love, fake love and causing others pain was away to quell my own or at least it's the sick cycle I was trapped in.

As I have done my best to gather the hearts of mankind's interest into the truth I've expressed so far it would be for naught if you fell to hear my word's purpose. I only speak the truth to destroy the lies that have been intricately woven into the seems. Please don't get lost in the madness or allow my truth to shock your conscious in a way that enables you to act. I have not offered this nor do I offer the following for your judgment. I do so in hopes of it inspiring you to help in saving the likes of me that still wallow in misery. They mean only to cry but their tear ducts have dried up and out of desperation mixed with rage they have created a character in which they are lost.

Long before I could put words together to express pain, I still felt a need to express pain. I'm forever remorseful for the sins in which I did and I could easily add more shocking stories of my dysfunctional coping skills in the hood. However I will end with my most noteworthy, not that I'm proud of either of them. I simply owe those most affected the truth as it was not as it was perceived nor manipulated by the editors that came way too late to have a clue.

Contrary to the belief of the many that shoot in judgment over those like me, there is no DNA or crime scene recreation that could ever capture the hearts or lack thereof of men, in my case a boy. You can't go to school, no matter how priced it is or how great the teacher is, to figure out my kind. You must walk in my shoes if you are too judge me right, if not you will always get it wrong.

December 1994 with Christmas just a few short weeks away I was peaking in my trade as a drug dealer. I had finally started to figure it out, money was no longer elusive and I was gaining ground. I was still doing things that didn't coincide with my goals or the person I wanted to be and I started doing some thinking. This was new for me, in the past my thinking was always attached to scheming. Now I was thinking in a way that was more constructive.

I had a child on the way Nicole was six months pregnant from our stolen moment we had shared. Her parents had zero faith in us being able to do right by a child at such young ages. For her they felt like she was naïve, too young and lacked the overall abilities to provide all a child needs. For me it was even more, on top of all the same concerns it was pretty obvious to them that I was a criminal. Her father pointed many things out to me and I had every right answer. I made all sorts of empty promises I didn't have the ability to keep.

I said I would get out the streets get a job, I would pay for everything and would always be there for my child. They didn't believe me I'm sure of it but reluctantly they allowed us to keep the child after my passionate pleas. Fast forward to December, I started to reflect on all the broken promises as my child was soon to be born. Yes I had provided financial aid, I had come running to Nicole side every time she called. However I would come on the dime of drug money, I had not got out the streets, school had not seen me. I was on a path to not always be there or be there at all.

For the first time I had really started to think of more than just myself. All of a sudden I wanted to live and actually had a reason to. I started to realize all the lives that were in the balance of the poor decisions I was making. I got apprehensive and lost my edge, my edge had been the way I was able to convince everyone including myself that I had nothing to lose and that death would be welcomed by me. This was no longer true in my warped mind, I had a child on the way. I had gone shopping already, I felt alive again and full of hope.

I started to second guess things, I became more aware of what I had rather than what I wanted. I wasn't rich but for a sixteen year old kid I was doing okay. I was the owner of three cars, jewelry and money. These were things that I had taken for granted because they were readily available. In fact I had money that I hadn't even counted yet. Jennifer and I were about to move into a house in a upper class neighborhood. I had things and many more coming in. this no longer meant as much to me as it had six months ago. So I started looking for my exit strategy, I secretly wanted out. I was done with this act I just didn't know how to close the curtain and exit the stage right.

My character and the reputation had become bigger than the creator of it and it had a mind of it's own. There was no way it would allow me to walk away, God knows I tried. Unfortunately the character was much more of the world than me, it knew that law that when two exist in one space one of them had to die so the other could live. I was trying to resurrect the humanity in me but the beast simply refused to die. The beast had already done and said things that I could not take back. The bell had been rung and there was no way to change the consequences of that. My poor choices as a mad man had set my stage, I had cast all my supporting roles to be fools just like me and this is how it played out.

On December 14, 1994 as Jennifer and I were sneaking presents out the trunk of the cars at 104 Landon street so we could wrap them. We were having a great night, I promised her I wasn't going anywhere that night. I had been in the streets a great deal selling drugs around the clock to pay for Christmas and to pay for the move into our new home. So she was on my back telling me to slow down. I told her that it was over, I was done and would be taking it easy until after the holidays. What she didn't know was that I really planned to be done all together, I just needed to figure out plans for a alternative income. I had ideas, we had options, one of which was she was almost a college graduate. I planned to send her back to school and do the same. I also could work with my father, I just needed to repair our strained relationship.

On this day this was my mindset, I was full of hope for a much better future. Then unknown to me my future was being planned by others in a completely different way. This guy name Ice who had just come home from prison was dating my cousin Ebony, he had another guy I knew name Tommy, my friend Terrell brother. A guy I knew name Teeter and some others I didn't know were planning a robbery. They planned to rob a house that they knew to be the residence of a drug dealer and his family. A recent verbal exchange took place between Ice and the brother of the drug dealer that left Ice with enough of a excuse to put this night in motion. No doubt it was likely a thought prior to it but in the hood we look for any little thing to motivate us and the argument was just که.

I got involved through Ice as a afterthought because my cousin Monique who knew his face was inside the home. She was there doing hair and house sitting. Ice wanted her gone thinking she would see his face and identify him. So he came to 104 Landon told me their plans and to go get my cousin out the house. I initially refused and advised him to wait. A true citizen would have been shocked by what Ice had revealed, I was not one. Despite my desires I was still a street kid so I responded as one then went back in the house.

I had noticed the person outside in the car that was with Ice was Tommy. I didn't know Ice nor did I know Teeter reputation, I only knew Ice through Ebony and Teeter through my boy Terrell. However I did know the reputation of Tommy, he was a hot head and he would easily shoot someone over the least bit of provocation. This troubled me and against the protest of Jennifer I got my gun as I never left home without it since the age of thirteen. I went outside and agreed I would go get Monique and that's it.

However at this time Snapper and Monet pulled up, they all knew each other and as the plan was revealed they wanted to be involved. This changed the dynamics and involved me due to my shaky loyalties to them. In my heart I was done but I was still in character. I had yet to destroy the character so I was two people at once and only a mad man could operate this way.

I agreed to get Monique out the house and to hold down my cousin and Monet. I went to get my cousin Monique and upon her coming to the porch she refused to leave. I planned to walk her across the street as they went in the house. I had no intent to return or assist them besides holding Snapper and Monet down after the fact. Which was more related to all unknown elements involved they didn't know about. A robbery can turn into a second robbery afterwards or worse, there was no honor amongst thieves so my assistance was to them in the aftermath.

Monique changed all my silly spur of the moment plans because she refused to leave and the house was all of a sudden rushed by these men while we argued on the porch. She ran behind them clearly thinking I was involved and had some influence over these men. I had absolutely none and easily could have turned into a victim if I made one wrong move.

I followed her inside things sped out of control. I was doing my best to ride the fence of not being involved but not looking like it to the assailants. I went from one role to another the entire time making me appear to the victims to be sick, diabolical and the man in charge. The absolute truth is, as I confess without reservations or a filter. Having zero fear of prosecution as I'm all out of a means to appeal a case I'm convicted of. A crime I have been incarcerated for since January 5, 1995. I went there that night because I had a feeling if I didn't Monique would be shot because of my refusal.

That was my purpose my sole reasoning for going out my door that night. I loved my family especially her, she was one of my favorite cousins. I did not want her blood on my hands so I went to get her knowing Tommy might shoot her just to make a point to me not to refuse him. I know how guys like him thinks, I was one of them. Sadly my decision to save her lead to me being here and she helped put me here proving no good deed goes unpunished.

   Let me be clear as I played both sides in that house I was no angel and I did more than enough to appear just as guilty as the rest of them. I won't allow this history to be rewritten by my bias. I did act just as criminally as they did that night. In fact I actually shot a man because he looked up at me, I shot him in his hand and I regret doing so.

   When these guys learned that there was no money to locate in the home and that the person they thought had kept his money there actually moved out they decided to take his son. Monique grabbed him refused to let him go, she was on the verge of being shot. She had already been given liberties she would not have had if not for me however she was about to lose it. This would have ended badly for all of us. So I quickly did my best to defuse the situation, I took him from her myself.

   I walked him out at gun point and as we separated from the men a little I told him I had no control of the situation. I really didn't, I had known him all our lives, he was a friend and I had lived in his home. This was wrong on so many levels and I wanted him to know I was not behind this. I see how my words would fall on deaf ears as I had a gun out taking him from his home at one in the morning.

   The facts are much more complicated than they seemed at the moment. I could have let him go right then some have said, others say we could have run off together. No one stopped to consider all the dangers to these options, my family lived all up and down that street. My door to my place where Jennifer and the kids were was open, they were vulnerable. The person I had come to save was still in danger. I had no logical options that at sixteen I could come up with in sixty seconds. I'm sorry but I just failed on every level and I'm paying for it.

I Confess

I made a effort after all these men were far away from my home and my family to get the boy away from them. I snuck to the trunk of the car he was being held in, got him out and tried to start the car to leave. The car battery would not turn the car over to start because the heat was on while the engine was off. I got caught with him in the passenger seat trying to start the car. I had no gun out on him, I was desperately trying to escape with him to make this situation right. We got caught and this part of the truth was never told. The district attorney decided to bury it and the victim thinking I did too little too late had no problem going along with this.

Yeah I was not a saint and I did many bad things even did some that very night but the truth is much more complex than the version of record. I don't know how guilty I was in the crimes of kidnapping my friend all I know for sure is I also made efforts that night to save him and I would like to think I actually played a role in him making it home without a scratch.

Exactly seven days later I was hiding out at my other girlfriend Nyree house due to the kidnapping incident. I was trying to figure out how to get myself out this mess and get the peace back that I was feeling as I was planning my exit out the life of crime. I was extremely stressed and the reason I was at Nyree house was because no one knew how to reach me. No one knew her address at all the only way to contact me was my pager which I wasn't answering.

On the morning of December 22, 1994 I was out of it, I was dead to the world. I had been up and on edge for days, sleep finally claimed me so I was out. Nyree kept trying to wake me up telling me someone was paging me. I did not care until she kept bugging me. I finally returned the unknown page by calling the number. It was my cousin shady who had just come home from jail, Snapper and Monet. They were all on Landon and Jennifer would not let them in the house which she was not supposed to. I didn't know why they were there in the first place.

They told me to come over that way it was urgent and I was very reluctant. I was avoiding Landon at the time, I was wanted by the police for the incident that had taken place on the fourteenth and into the morning of the fifteenth. I eventually agreed to come and I called a cab instead of using a known car.

When I got there they told me that they called a guy we all did drug deals with, used my name and the code for him to bring drugs over. The plan was to rob him for drugs and money then make him take them to his stash. I was pissed! I wanted no part in this especially at my house where all the this drama had taken place just seven days earlier. I knew it was a mistake when I first decided to stay here with Jennifer and the kids until our house was ready. I had rules against people knowing where I live, especially when people I wanted to protect were there. I made a serious error and it was costing me.

The person I was, he would never think twice and he would be prepared for anything. I was no longer him, my character had changed in my heart but no one had got that memo including the fool in me. This hesitation stole my edge and made it inevitable that I would make mistakes. All the lessons I had learned would not resonate until I was years removed from freedom.

I had become a leader with my edge, there was no one that would try to lead me. I was my own person and although I was far from a man, I had taken my manhood. In a sick twisted way when the moment I started to retreat, my edge was lost, simultaneously allowing the small window of this seven day period to make me a follower. I could have easily controlled those moments that changed my life if I still had my careless attitude, not having it actually worked against me in the end. This was no coincidence and I learned valuable life lessons because of it.

This drug dealer was on his way with the drugs he thought I wanted. I could have easily paid for them, I actually had the money and that would not have hurt me at all. What no one knew was that I had gained my lost ground back. I didn't have the countless hundred dollar bills that I had in Jersey but I was not far off and had I wanted to press forward I was on pace to blow past even that. So the petty drugs he was coming over with were something I could have covered but I wasn't thinking as a leader. I was trying to serve two mindsets, two hearts and the ruler of my actions was still the created character. I was still far away from the person I wanted to transition to, so I killed my dreams of change and lived out my reality.

The person I was at the time was heartless, I had no real value for human life. There was no value of my own life so there was no way I could place value on anyone else life. It is the character that I owned when a guy I dealt with pulled up. I told all the people in the house I was playing for keeps. For me it was always all or nothing so I let them know that my involvement meant this man was about to die. There was no middle ground, it was the only way out for me, this would be my final act and I meant to make it one that would make those present never come calling for Lil Dee.

Snapper had seen me in the past live out my words, he knew I was going all the way and he backed out. His cab pulled up at the same time as the man arrived for our drug transaction. He spoke to him and he left knowing he was one of the main reasons this man was about to die. He had made the call after all and it was just as much his plan as theirs, leave or not the blood would still be on his hands too.

The man was told by Monet to come in and told him I was in the kitchen as Shady hid in the bathroom. Jennifer and the kids were in the room, the kids were sleep and Jennifer was doing her best to play sleep. When the man came to the door of the kitchen I shot him in the legs and stood over him as Monet and Shawn approached. I asked him where his stash house was, he kept saying the address but I could not understand what he was saying and shot him again to force him to answer.

I was out of my mind and I had no feelings at all, to me this last thing was in my way of getting out of this life, someone had to die so that I could live. I had no idea that the person that needed to die was the monster inside of me that I had created out of pain and fear. I took all my pain, confusion and desperation out through the actions that were taking place.

Did anyone else shoot, contribute to the death of this man, yes they did but just as in the kidnapping case, I was the only one charged. I'm the only one doing time and made to account for that day. So I will leave their details to be told by them if they ever choose to do so. I will own the fact that I did shoot him, I did play a major role in the death of this man who I'm sure is loved and deeply missed.

As I stated when I spoke on the shooting death of Steve, a killer has no idea how many lives are in the balance. Sorry is simply never enough. It does absolutely nothing to fill the void. So I will not waste my time or theirs telling how sorry I am. I find it better to instead do my best to prevent some little confused child, out of pain to cause a family the same pain I caused to others and to my own.

Many people's lives changed from my careless behavior. There were so many people forced to hurt because my own pain went undetected and I was too cowardice to deal with it. Instead as most frightened cowards do I chose to lash out, masking my pain by pretending to be above being hurt. We are all humans, we all hurt and when you see a kid acting as if he or she is above it, it's likely the kid is me. There is no doubt the kid is hurting so try to appeal to the pain and the healing process opposed to allowing that child to destroy themselves. So many lives are in the balance of how we deal with that child's pain. Please if you dare to judge, dare to save.

Confessions of The Accused

Chapter 13

Welcome back to Buffalo

·

After the shooting my life really spun out of control, I went on the run, I was on it since I was twelve, and I simply didn't get it. Jennifer had left before I did, she took the kids back to Pennsylvania with her parents.

I left a few days later, the day before Christmas. I headed to Bradford, I wasn't planning on staying, I wanted to help Jennifer get settled with the kids. Then I planned to go to Seabrook New Hampshire where I had a lady friend no one knew about.

None of these things fell into place because Jennifer never met me in Bradford, forcing me to travel to chase after her. I should have worried about myself, but I wasn't thinking. I had lost my edge and I was completely off balance when it came to self-preservation.

Subsequently I was arrested in route to bring Jennifer back to Bradford and six days after the arrest I was being driven back to Buffalo by two homicide detectives. Once they got me back to Buffalo I was arrested for kidnapping in the first degree and I was told I'd soon be charged with murder as well.

The charges they'd forgotten to mention should have been the first on their list. I should have been charged with a hate crime. I hadn't just hurt others, I hurt myself and I did so out of hate. I had destroyed the life and the future of the boy in me who wanted to be a fireman. My motive was hatred, I hated what I allowed to happen to me and I hated what I allowed my response to be to it, so I destroyed my life. As much as I'd hurt others, it was lost on the arresting officers, and those who followed just how much I'd hurt myself, as well as the reason why.

After my arrest and arraignment there were a million revelations all at once. The first was who my true family and friends were. The list was shockingly small and the people to actually show up were mostly those least expected to. They were also people who could've easily treated me the way I'd treated them.

My first visit was actually from this girl name Sonya, she was a young girl I was dealing with. She was actually my age but in comparison to the women in my life she was young, too young to be coming into a visiting room alone. The rules were you had to be eighteen or older unless accompanied by a adult. She had used a family members ID. The thing was, I'd just got to Buffalo, no one but my mother was aware I was in custody besides Jennifer. So to get a visit from her was shocking, I actually walked past her table thinking she was there for someone else. She hadn't heard from me and she was worried, she told me she'd been calling the jail everyday with my name, and as soon as I got there she'd written me, as well as come to visit.

This was significant in many ways because it showed me what care and concern looked like. It also gave me a measuring stick for those who could not care any less, and there was plenty. In fact it was some of them had actually assured that I would be there with their own slithering tongue. The truth was, I had invested in fear and when your facing life in prison with no way of ever getting out, fear fades quickly.

My house was robbed by my very own family, I was getting pictures from Angie who turned out to be a true friend and people in the pictures she'd sent of a party were wearing my clothes. These were my clothes, no one in the city of Buffalo owned these clothes I'd never worn. Now I knew who robbed my house and it was family, this ripped at my heart strings.

Soon after that the letters from Angie started slowing up and I learned from her that Shady beat her up and accused her of sleeping with me while he was in jail. Told her to stop writing me and took the money from her she had to help me out with my legal defense. The revelations of who was who became very clear real quick.

It seemed overnight my life had changed, Nyree came, she made sure I had underclothes and told me not to worry she'd stand by me through this. The following week she was in my face in tears, she was told by my own friends, and family that I'd robbed her house for kids toys. They told her I had aids, and told her to leave me alone. Then tried to come on to her, this was Monet and Snapper, they were partners. I was crushed and despite my efforts, we couldn't salvage our relationship at all, so Nyree and I were over.

The list of things that took place were killing my spirit, the only hope I had, my one bright spot was my unborn child. This was all I had in the end, the money, the friends, most of my family, it was all gone. The things were all gone, and the one sure joy I had was the child that I'd betrayed the most.

Here I sat in prison, with charges that could give me twenty five years to life, and other charges not yet filed where I could get fifty more years. I had been so caught up that I was losing sight of what was true. I kept it real with the streets, I was about to do time for the streets, but I'd left a kid in the streets, and only God knew how that would turn out.

Pretty soon it was time for trial, things had settled down about the other possible charges. My only case was the kidnapping case and I was thinking, "as crazy as the truth sounded, it was still the truth", so I had a chance. I just needed the truth to come out, if it did I was sure I could end up going home.

This didn't happen, no one told the truth, at least not the one I knew. They told their version of it and made me look guilty. Hindsight says I was a fool to think otherwise, I mean here I was telling my side, with a mixture of lies, not really telling the entire story, and also not trying to reveal the names of the people involved. I looked like a idiot, no one could believe these guys didn't know me, or vice versa, no one could believe that things played out anywhere close to how I said. The fact of the matter is, I was lying too much, I was being loyal to the streets and that loyalty cost me a lot, it always does.

I was found guilty as charged on all counts except for possession of a firearm. I was headed to state prison for a long time, possibly the rest of my life. I had lived all of sixteen years on the street and now here I was about to spend my best years in a cage. I could cry, but deep down I knew I had chased down this fate and regardless of what I said, I deserved to be in the position I'd finally achieved.

On January 31, 1996 I was sentenced to eighteen years to life. I was seventeen years old and I was now a lifer, there was no way out, I was going to prison. I went back to my cell that night not knowing what year it would be when I went to the parole board to beg for a second chance at life. All I knew was that I was a fool, I started to think of how I had gotten to that point. I retraced my steps, took note of all my travels, I asked myself was it worth it, and I needed no answer, my heart was clear, it wasn't.

I failed myself and I knew it. Despite whatever had been done to me, I failed myself. I could blame whoever I wanted to, whatever would help me sleep at night. At the end of my list of excuses, I had failed to show up for myself in all those places that others had failed me.

I allowed what was done to me to be an excuse when it should have been my reference of how not to treat me, and how not to treat others. God blessed me with knowing what hurt at an early age. I had a duty to make sure I used it as a point of reference, instead I used it as a crutch and as a excuse to fail, which I did perfectly.

In my heart I knew that I failed, I knew I'd hurt people. Somewhere I had a man's mother crying, I had my mother crying. I had Nicole's mother crying for what her kid was about to face trying to raise our

I Confess

daughter alone, and I had Nicole crying, not knowing what she'd tell De'aira when she wanted her daddy. There was no taking any of it back and I knew my road was long, and my lessons would continue to learned the hard way. Sadly I found myself alone, at that time I didn't even believe in God, so I didn't even have that to lean on.

I balled myself up, threw the cover over my head and tried to cry, no tears would come, my tear ducts hadn't been used in years. I'd forgotten how to cry, or I didn't have the ability to do so. I don't know, maybe I was in my character and I didn't care. So instead I did as I've done many nights since I was a child, I fought for and against sleep. I wanted to sleep but was afraid to go. I was a mess, and sadly I was in a place that no one cared. If I thought I'd gone unnoticed before, I hadn't seen anything yet.

A few days passed, mask still in place, no need to remove it now, I'm going to need it. So I held on for dear life and braced myself for the unknown. Before I leave I want to get a visit, I planned to see my sexy trooper. Sonya, despite the odds had been a main stay, everyone else had done the amazing disappearing act. As we planned to see each other the next night after, "when she get's her home pass from the group home she's in", the guard calls me. I hang up to go see what he wants.

Pack up, you're going off property to state prison, my heart dropped and my mask falls to the floor. I had just got sentenced, it's night time, all my protest meant nothing. I'm state property and they'd come to collect. The thirteen months I'd been in county I'd been a handful. I had assaults on staff and I even had a pending felony for assaulting a sergeant. I had done my share of adolescent behavior. They wanted me out of their facility and tonight was as good a night as any.

Just as quickly as Buffalo had welcomed it's native son back, it had prosecuted me, and now it was time to say goodbye. I made my last phone call, gave all my things away, picked my mask up, and put it back on with the fake smile attached. Then I left and only a fool is heartless in the face of the unknown. I had been a fool, but I was a fool no more, I was scared, mostly scared I'd never get another chance at life.

Derrel Moore

Confessions of the accused

Chapter 14

A kid in the big house

The following morning before sunrise I was escorted by van, "which was why they told me to pack up my things the night before", and took me to a isolation court hold tank. This drove me crazy all night, I had never seen them take someone upstate this way.

The trip was nerve wrecking and long, I felt like I was leaving the country instead of driving three hours away. When the van pulled up in front of Elmira correctional facility it was worse than I'd imagined. It looked like a old castle where you could go in but it was unlikely you'd ever come out. We walked through the front and I had to pass an old statue with two naked boys. The inscription said something to the reference of, "you come in a boy and leave out a man, only the strong survive". If I was nervous before, I was completely terrified now and I hadn't even seen the inside of the place. The processing was degrading and I wasn't just stripped of my dignity as I was processed in, they also stripped me of my name literally. Somehow my paperwork had been written wrong and my real name was written as my alias. Despite my protest that my name was not Derrell Austin, my real name was Derrel with one L, and my last name was Moore I was ignored. I never used the name I now was told was my real name as long as I was state property. So I had to learn a new name plus remember my state number. I was coming in the big house with absolutely nothing, and no one.

I wish for the sake of seeming very strong and extraordinary I could say I was unmoved. That I got inside and was the toughest guy on the cell block. Then the other, much more compassionate side of me wishes I could say, "for the sake of those my actions hurt", that I was tortured, beaten by other prisoners and raped. Maybe that might ease the pain of those who my actions caused pain that I can't even imagine.

Truth is, my fears were actually worse than what was awaiting me. In fact most of my hardships I'd eventually encounter, besides the obvious, was all self-inflicted. I was my own worse enemy, I had been for several years and it would take some growing up before that would change.

Prison for a kid my age, with my issues was the worst possible place for me. The problem is, it was the most appropriate place to be under the circumstances, and what was available in the state of New York. Under the law, at sixteen I was considered a adult. I couldn't buy a drink if I was free, and even in state custody I was unable to purchase cigarettes. State law says you must be eighteen to purchase cigarettes. I was too young , just old enough to get life in prison, but too young to have the capacity to reason when it comes to smoking although my cellmate could give me some.

I learned very fast that most prison rules made no sense, in fact the main rule in prison was that the policies can't make sense. We could purchase all the can food we want in prison commissary, weapons for sale, buy as many as you can afford to, but if you allow your finger nails to grow too long you'd get a misbehavior report and put on lock down. Supposedly you can use your nails as weapons, so you can buy all the weapons you want, just don't grow your nails to scratch someone with.

This was my new home and I just had a very rough start because I simply couldn't adjust, to be honest more than two decades have past and I still struggle with it, so at seventeen it was simply impossible. I spent close to six months in reception before I was sent to my first facility, I was sent to the adolescent capital, a place called Coxsackie correctional facility. I had heard about the prison, I had heard the kids were wild, the place was six hours from Buffalo, and the list went on. I didn't care where it was, nor how wild the prison population was, what scared me or what turned me off was the fact that the prison had no trailer visits. I had to live in prison, I had no interest in going to a facility to spend my life with no trailer visits while every other maximum security prison at that time had trailer visits. I didn't understand and didn't have any interest in trying.

The first day I was there and was released for morning breakfast run to the mess hall, I cut myself and told the prison staff I didn't know who did it. They didn't believe me and I didn't care, they could put me in segregation or protective custody, it didn't matter to me, just get me out this place and they did.

The funny thing is I was having too many behavioral problems, even once they moved me I was always in trouble and the first thing you we had to do to get a trailer was stay out of trouble. I hadn't really thought this thing through at all.

I just couldn't buy into the logic of the staff running the prison. I was assigned to a facility program, "custodial maintenance", which was trying to teach me to sweep and mop the proper way. The problem for me was the law library was right next door, and I had a life sentence. I wasn't the smartest idiot in the facility, but I knew enough to know I was in the wrong room. So I'd get caught out of place in the law library, when I was supposed to be learning how to use a mop ringer. It sounds funny, but at seventeen with a life sentence, and a one year old daughter it was hard for me to get the joke.

So I'd get put on lockdown, do my time, and they'd send me right back to this program to learn to mop. In my heart, I felt it was going against my very nature to fight back and protect myself to sit in that room. I couldn't live with myself if I really sat there trying to learn how to use cold water to mop with instead of going next door to find out about my constitutional rights violations. So I would go and I'd get locked down again. I wasn't breaking, lockdown meant nothing to me in comparison to what I was using as my motivator. I was eventually assigned a new program outside that building, far away from the law library.

Had I been a tad bit smarter, a bit older and a lot less angry at the world, I could've seen what I was doing was counter-productive. I was still a child, I had no visionary skills at all to see what I thought was best for me and I should have used my head. I was there in prison for my short sightedness. If I could tell that fool anything at all I would have warned him that he's his own worst enemy, to slow down, and listen. Unfortunately we learn as we live, which makes it impossible not to screw life up a bit as you go. I had done a serious number on myself already, and I wasn't done, in fact I was far from it.

After a few birthdays had passed me by in the big house, a failed marriage at eighteen that lasted about the same amount of time as Kim k, and Chris's did. I was all in, my heart had only grown colder as more disappointment occurred in my life. People made pit stops in my life as if I was an all night station. The one constant ,who never let time or distance come between our friendship was Angie. She took insults, suffered through assaults, and through it all she remains my friend. I can count her and God as my most unlikely main stays during these darkest days.

I have to clarify this, I was raised to believe in God but somewhere along the way I lost my faith. Then the more self-hatred I displayed the less I believed, and the guiltier I felt. Then it got so bad I was dead inside and had concluded that there was no God. When I found myself alone, yearning to pray, yearning to believe, my knees wouldn't bend. I was ashamed and afraid I'd done way too much wrong, so I simply avoided the thoughts of God. Then while at my worse, it was God alone that I knew beyond all doubt was there and true. My thoughts were that so bad concerning God that I was certain the rest of my life would be in a cage without God, so learning of God's mercy was something very remarkable that I didn't count on.

Sadly those I'd done unthinkable things for which displeased God were nowhere to be found. They were all gone and was God alone that sent mercy upon me in countless ways through countless people. I know beyond all doubt it was God sending certain people to stay for a season or two in my life. There were times I've gotten four and five letters at a time on a daily basis from Angie. Her words were inspiring, they encouraged me and helped me grow. She owed me nothing, this was God working through her, I'm certain she'd testify to that.

As people I loved would do things that caused me pain, worked to break my resolve causing me to grow even colder it was this balance that kept me at bay. I'd get to the edge, one foot and one arm off the cliff, and God would use someone to give me hope. I lived in between hopeless and hopeful, the room was small, the bed even smaller but I held on.

Nickie, the girl I fell in love with as a boy long before I knew what love was dropped into my life out of nowhere. This came right on time as I was feeling defeated in life. Her letter had the power to resurrect me, and make my spirit soar. We hadn't said more than five words to each other at one time in our entire lives and here she had written me a three page letter. I was alive, I felt like I still mattered, life wasn't over and people still cared. On top of that Nickie had wrote me, of all people, her.

We exchanged letters, promises and in a matter of seconds it seemed, we were in love, planning to marry. She was twenty, going on twenty-one and I was nineteen soon to be twenty. We were kids and prison was a old beast, we didn't stand a chance. We gave it a hell of a shot and I didn't make it easy as I was always in trouble.

I went to the box or commonly known as the hole in prison and I was sent to Upstate correctional facility, a new prison in New York state at that time. I was on one of the first buses to be sent there, we were a experiment. We had no medical, no law library, the place wasn't ready to house the states most troubled prison population as it had advertised. When Nickie came to visit the sight of me behind the caged like gate in front of her was too much for her. She refused to kiss me through the gate, before she left she made sure to let me know she wouldn't be back to see me there like a animal.

I did my box time and was moved to Sing Sing correctional facility, everyone thought I was supposed to be happy. All I could think about is the fact it was nine hours from home and no one would ever visit me there. I was scared to even tell Nickie where I was, I told her over the phone not to worry where I was at because I was leaving. I had a plan, it had worked before and I'd try again. She told me to just tell her where I was and stop acting crazy. I told her bracing myself for her words but she simply said she'd be there next week on her day off and she was.

I thought I was the man, I continued to get in trouble doing nothing to make a effort to get closer to home. I was running around that place like I was free. I was making money in there like I was in the streets. I had cash money like I was out on the block with no fear of being caught due to officer's being complicit. In the meantime I had no idea I was losing my relationship. I thought things were great until she didn't show up for our prison wedding.

I was crushed and it didn't make it better when one of my appeals for my case was denied that same week. I was devastated and I went off the deep end for a while. I had my mask on tight, I was back to not caring about anything. I even brought my comrade, "Tone G", back to life. I was the leader of the notorious gangster disciples in prison, and we were acting a fool in Sing Sing. I didn't care and I made sure all my recruits didn't either.

One day I got a visit from Nickie, she was still hanging around but all the signs were there and like I said my mask was on tight. When I got down there I wanted to impress her or maybe prove I didn't need her. I told her to meet this guy's girl in the bathroom, he owed me money but I didn't tell her this, I just said go see what she wants. When she returned she gave me a reality check that help me grow up a bit.

She refused to take the money from the girl, she told me I was a fool, said I'm still the same idiot I was before came in. She told me how she was working twelve hours a day to take care of me, her kids, and herself. All I had to do was stay out of trouble, instead I'm in there getting into more trouble. She told me she felt she was the only one in the relationship making sacrifices. That the least I could do was stay out of trouble and get moved closer to home. Instead I'm in here still being a damn criminal, then I'm trying to get her to do the same by taking drug money in a prison bathroom.

She was right and had I been ready to receive that heavy dose of reality maybe I would have stopped. I wasn't ready I kept going and it would be over four years before I would see Nickie again. I didn't know it but that wasn't just a speech it was a goodbye. My mask was an upgraded version, I had been waiting on her to leave, in my mind everyone left and she was no exception. I went even harder in my shell, I was touched by her words and her leaving but I buried that pain. I had a life sentence to DIE doing if I couldn't see her no more so what.

Yeah I hadn't changed if anything I was worse, I was angrier now. I found a new much longer list of people to blame and I was good at blaming people for how I treated myself.

After a bit more than two years I was kicked out of Sing Sing. When they kicked me out I was sick. I felt like I had just been arrested all over and put in prison. I wasn't in prison there, I was living like I was in the streets. I ate what I wanted, did what I wanted and had more money in my mattress then dudes had in the streets. The stories that have been told about that place has it's truth, most fools tell other peoples stories, bottom line I had fun although I was doing a life sentence and I'm certain someone somewhere is telling my story as their own.

Confessions of the accused

Chapter 15

She promised she'd always be there

When my mother was first diagnosed with lymphoma in 2002 I was devastated. She had finally started to enjoy her life despite my situation, my incarceration had been hard on her. I'm sure she blamed herself and there was nothing I could say to stop her from doing so.

My mother had gone through every level of drug addiction from the aspect of dealing and using. My own troubles only made it worse for her and provided a need to numb herself even more. This is how she dealt with whatever her personal demons were. So when her only child was facing being in prison forever her addiction got worse.

So when she moved to Atlanta and was doing her music again I was happy for her. She would send me pictures of herself performing all over the country. She even opened for Lenny Williams which was one of the happiest nights of her musical life. She had a music label with her husband called M.L.I. records, "music, life, intelligence". She put out her own original music and was in talks with major labels. As she started to enjoy it cancer came knocking, it was time for her to pay for all she had done to abuse her God given temple.

This had the power to break me especially when the doctors told her she likely had months to live. I didn't know how to deal with it and in fact I shut down, I blocked it out. Then the hospital stays became more frequent and her weight started to disappear by the second. God had my full attention and I begged, and begged, and begged.

Months turned into years, we had scare after scare. She would always pull through. My mother was a fighter after all, cancer was no match for this crazy lady. There were way too many things we still had to work out between us. Things needed saying we had made our fair share of mistakes that had hurt. We needed our moment and we kept putting it off because we believed God would give us tomorrow.

Almost five years after she was diagnosed she was put back in the hospital. A death bed visit was planned by her for me to come see her from prison. I was numb, this was my lady, she was the one I could always count on when I needed someone. The truth of the matter was she was the reason I could pretend not to care about anything or anyone.

When I got to the hospital I expected to see my mother with tubes all over her and unable to speak. That wasn't Darlene, she was up with the biggest most beautiful smiles you'd ever want to see. Hers was a smile you would pay her to show you and she had it on for me free of charge. I had no way of knowing it was a front and she was in pain. She was the lady I always needed her to be so that day in her mind would be no different no matter what it cost her.

There were no signs of a dying woman, we laughed, we joked, and we loved each other. All we had was a hour, she tried to feed me but all I wanted was to look at her. I had to be sure she was okay and this wasn't goodbye. She assured me it wasn't, told me she would see me again soon, she even pulled out a fist full of money, and said it was for me. She asked me could I take it or have someone come pick it up. I agreed I would have someone come get it, I wasn't really worried about money I was just glad she was okay.

I left happy I had seen her, happy she seemed okay and I was content for the moment. It didn't last but a second as I approached the elevators with escorting officer's from the prison, my mother called out my name loudly. She always had the loudest voice on the planet and she used it that day. I got this strange feeling it was goodbye that she was trying to say. All I know is that voice yelling my name in that hospital hall is stuck in my head. It was the very last words I heard from her. My mother died August 26, 2005 right before hurricane katrina and one half of me left with her.

The death of a parent is anticipated, it's the natural order of life, but I hadn't lived a natural life. I never anticipated her not being here. I didn't know what I was supposed to do without her. Life simply didn't make much sense without her.

I didn't know what message God was sending me, God knows my heart so why take her knowing I couldn't live without her? It was very hard and I was certain I was on borrowed time.

Between my father, my wife at the time Jasmine and Nickie who had just come back in my life, God used each to help me through. I had someone, sometimes all of them there every day. I was only twenty minutes from home at Wende correctional facility at the time. God had placed me there and I wasn't there for good behavior it was the mercy of the most high, my Savior.

I needed constant human contact so I could have something to hold on to. A few weeks after her death I had a trailer scheduled. It was perfect timing, I needed to get out of prison and I was dying inside. I went out there and for the first time since her death, I cried. In that two bedroom trailer I felt I could release my tears and I cried for my loss, but more for my regrets.

I had been a handful, I'd required way too much from her and I had given so little in return. I wanted a do over, I needed a second chance at being her son. I wanted to listen, be a good boy, go to school and make my mommy proud. All the things that I'd spit on, I wanted back, but I knew I'd never get a do over. Life isn't something you get to screw up then do over whenever you feel inspired to, no matter how bad you need or want it.

Jasmine let me cry, she provided the venue despite the pain I exposed her to. The thing is we were married, things were rocky, but we were pushing forward. Then out of nowhere Nickie shows up and throws us both for a loop. She told me she had a baby, I forgave her and I forgave the last four years she had been a no show.

This put me at odds with my wife, it broke my heart but it also gave her permission to walk away as she had been begging to do. The emotions of all of us were raw and with the death of my mother it intensified. Things went back and forth, there were days when Jasmine wanted to stay in our relationship, and in my heart I knew she deserved better. I knew I had to let her go although I didn't want to. At the same time I knew there was unfinished business with Nickie in my heart, but I also knew it was only a matter of time for us, yet I had to try. On the tail end of my mother's death I had filed for a divorce to free a woman from me that I loved enough to let go. The situation I had pulled her into was killing her spirit, I was killing her spirit and I no longer recognized her. Soon after my divorce Nickie and I were married. We had rushed into it, we both pretended it was okay since we knew each other since we were kids, we wanted to believe it so we did.

I was so caught up in all the self-made drama around me that I was able to pretend I had not just lost my mother. Then I was shocked back into reality when my Granny Love's health took a turn for the worse. Before I knew it, I was in the same hospital on the same floor I was just on nine months previously. It took all my will power as I walked past the door of the room I had visited my mother in not to run in there to see if she was sitting in that bed with her smile. My knees actually buckled as I tried to pass and I still regret not being able to go check.

My Granny Love was in bad shape, my uncle Robert and my Grandfather was there by her side, my grandfather would not leave his wife's side and you could tell he was in deep agony. When I walked in Robert left to give me time with her. My grandfather stayed with me and his wife trying to get her to understand who I was.

At first she thought I was my mother, she missed her smart loud mouth child and it showed. Then she realized it was me and tried to move as if she could get up. She couldn't but she started saying that she had to listen to what the doctors said so she could get out of there and home to me. She thought her grand baby was free. I couldn't tell her otherwise. She was crying tears of joy and frustration, her baby was free but now she was confined.

I took this time to tell her words she needed to hear in order to let go in peace and words I needed to say in order to do the same. Like I said when two exist in the same space in conflict with each other, one has to die so that the other can live in peace. It was time to live but first I had to destroy the beast and that beast was my excuses.

That day I told my Granny Love the truth, "Granny Love none of it is your fault, you did the very best you could, you were a great mom as well as a great Granny Love to me, you did not fail us, our actions are not your fault". I thanked her for loving me even when I didn't deserve it. I told her I loved her, then she struggled to ask me a question and gave me sound advice I'll forever cherish. Then I told her she had done a great job and she could rest knowing she was a great woman. I told her the truth and it was time I started to own it, not just what she had been but the choices I made. She thanked me for my words and I knew it was goodbye.

I left in tears, I didn't hide them, I took them with me proudly. I knew I would never see this sweet loving woman ever again, not unless I started paying back some of what I owed. She had no doubt earned her way into heaven and if I ever wanted to see my Granny Love again I had some work to do.

When I got back to the prison a peace came over me, the two pillars of my life were gone. It was time for me to put my big boy pants on, I could do one of two things, I could grow up and live the life I was created for or I could fold. It was time to prove how tough I was. I had shown that I could be a coward and take a life. Now was time to prove I was capable of giving life and I had to start with myself.

My mother had broken a promise she never had the power to keep.

The lesson was clear, there is only one certainty which is God. We all live according to God's will, we can waste our days doing nothing going nowhere making excuses for it or destroy the excuses and live.

  I chose to live, I didn't bury my Granny Love or my mother. They live in my heart, what I did bury was my demons. I was done being the victim of others and especially the victim of myself. The tortured boy in me could only be vindicated by the man I could be. So I chose to rebuild myself, I chose to live regardless of where on earth my physical body happen to be.

Confessions of the accused

Chapter 16

Devastation inspired change

It was when I was at my worse, me against the worst enemy I ever had, with all the excuses I needed to quit that I found my humanity again. I had used every excuse I could my entire life in order to rationalize my bad behaviors.

With the two most important women in my entire life deceased, the woman I loved and supposed soulmate cheating on me yet again. I had more than enough excuses readily available and my pattern would have been to use those excuses. Breaking the pattern would prove difficult I struggled with my mighty arsenal of examples of nothingness. I had regressions, I dealt with doubts, but I pressed ahead.

As the visiting of my wife would falter and that familiar look became more present in her eyes I refused to fold. I pretended not to see it, but unlike my past, I didn't pretend not to care. Instead I started to realize that hurt people find ways to hurt other people and she was a woman rooted in pain. I realized I was able to see this because I was too.

We eventually split again and predictably she resurfaced with yet another child. As much as I loved her I knew that the two of us could never be, not that we didn't try again, and again. I will simply say and Pray all those that matter will understand, I thank God for all the lessons which ultimately turned out to be blessings.

One can imagine a man coming into the system has a laundry list full of reasons to be broken. You couple that with all the loss along the way and sprinkle in his childhood trauma. You have the perfect recipe for a well-made monster.

If not for the mighty protection and mercy of God I'd be exactly that. I would be completely broken and dare anyone to walk my path without ending up the same or worse.

I must stress that it is only by God's will that I still exist. By God's hands I was fashioned to take each step I took and come out the other end to call attention to the lost. I beg you to get involved as a parent, a relative, even a friend or advocate. I wanted more for my life, I needed more and as God has proven to me, I deserved more.

However for me it took losing everything I thought I could never live without before I was able to wake up and recognize my own worth. There is simply no way we can allow devastation to be our children's wake up call. The truth is for many that devastation is their death, for others it's two and three decades in prison.

This could not be the ideal fate Ms. Harriet Tubman had for us as she marched the likes of us from slavery to freedom. How her spirit must quake at the many that have been broken by poverties whip. How the Martin's, the Malcolm's, Marcus Garvey and the Mighty Mandela's of our history must agonize over our failings.

Whose fault is it really when a child terrorizes his own neighborhood? Whose duty is it to stop him, heal him and guide him back to the love of self? When is it ever his fault alone?

As one of the very troubled out the flock I don't contend to have all the answers. Yet I do know we, "my kind", do care. We lie when we say we don't, we will be counted as good if you call us to it.

Once I found myself all alone in this world I was forced to dig deep. I started to truly self-analyze and get to know myself in ways I never had. For as long as I could remember I had been running and hiding. I had shut the world out and I quickly realized that included myself.

I was shocked by what I started to learn. I realized pretty quick that I was much more than I thought. I had sold myself short with the label I had placed on myself. I didn't even know I was actually handsome, funny and a intelligent person. I was insecure and didn't know it. I had imagined that my criminal behaviors were the sum of the whole. I had never before looked in the mirror and seen what others did.

In my mind I was a animal, I wasn't worth much at all and I'd acted like it. Yes I had been called handsome, yes I had been given reassuring compliments. However I had never received them as authentic. I was my own worst enemy and I had worked a number on myself.

I kept digging and I was finding gold. Yes I found some baggage, things I didn't like and needed to address. However I was learning that I was worth a lot more than I thought and a lot more than I had sold myself for. The pennies I had chased after, destroyed lives for, shattered friendships over, all of it, even the pain I used as a excuse would forever be incapable of being my equal.

The more I found my true worth the more remorse I felt for all my actions. Previously I was only sorry I had been caught now I was forced to take a hard look at my actions. I wanted to say to my victims that I was sorry but realized in most cases it would be impossible. Many of them were unknown to me, I had hurt so many without any real regard at all, I didn't keep a record. There was no way I'd be able to speak to the deceased and say sorry. Saying it to the family meant nothing when I had nothing substantive to accompany it.

I took my troubled heart to God for comfort, I found direction was attached to the sanctuary. There was simply no way I could ever change my past. There was also no way I could ignore it and live in some alternative reality. I had to take ownership of all it's parts if I was ever to truly obtain the redemption I'm seeking.

In the midst of this struggle is when, fifteen years removed from society, on March 9, 2009 I got a visit from a cold case detective. I was being housed in Dannemora New York at Clinton correctional facility. He was here for a murder case, the one I previously mentioned.

I always knew eventually someone would come and secretly I was glad to finally face it. I soon learned I would do so alone. Everyone involved had blamed every detail on me. I looked at each statement the detective had against me and I knew I had left quite the impression. There were statements from people who knew me my entire life and each one had got it wrong. I was unknown and I had to deal with it.

At first I wanted to fight the case, I knew I was not the person I had been painted as. So I refused to just accept the terms that were being offered to me. I wasn't really fighting what was, I was fighting for the person I was struggling to become.

Eventually a court order was issued to the State and I was turned over to the custody of Erie County in Buffalo New York. I was back in the holding center after fifteen years. The place smelled the same, it was filled with the stench of hopelessness, urine, feces, throw up, and blood mixed together then painted on the walls. When I was given my ID name tag bracelet it had my real name on it. Here I could be who my parents had named me and I protested. I was Derrell Austin now, I didn't even know if most of my family and friends would know me by my real name. the guards refused to allow me to be held under a alias so I was forced after all those years to adjust again. This proved to be a problem for my family, they kept coming to visit me and being told there was no Derrell Austin in custody.

They thought I was giving them the wrong location of where I was being held. Then they concluded that I was losing my mind finally. It took days for all of us to realize Derrel Moore was back in existence. I had been so far removed from reality for almost two decades that even I didn't know my own name.

After months of fighting over what was in order to protect what could be, my attorney and I had a long talk. He told me he could absolutely win the case and he wanted to fight it. I no longer did and told him so. I gave him several lame excuses about being tired of being in the county jail, the treatment, the food and the inmates that were using unorthodox tactics in becoming jailhouse informants, creating cases on innocent people.

To his credit he ignored all my excuses, deemed them the nonsense they were and said if you did it, you can plead guilty, if not we fight it. I chose not to fight, I was tired and chose to take the plea. I took my time and the person I was starting to become did my best to apologize to the family for the person I had been.

Guilty! Those empty words meant nothing to them as I knew they wouldn't. I had nothing else that they could hold against me or on to that was worth a morsel to the pain I had caused. On top of it, the time I was sentenced to seemed to be without consequence to them. They had no idea the true price I had already paid for my actions. I had been paying two times the amount of a king's ransom for many years and I knew from talks with my conscious I would be paying the rest of my life.

I left the holding center knowing I had no more outstanding debts to pay by way of the criminal justice system. That would be my last time in criminal court, I also knew it wasn't the highest court of the land. I still would be judged some day in my entirety by God. Knowing this I took the long ride back to the prison constantly thinking of that day.

I started to think in terms of legacy, how I could transition from my poor start to my great finish. I wanted to be able to make the case to the most high that when I knew better I actually did do much better. So I had to figure out a way to get and stay out my own way when it counted the most. This would prove difficult in a cage where great thoughts came attached to heart wrenching regret.

The more I healed, the greater my ideals became and as this occurred the cell closed in and my regret grew thick. I had to figure out how to manage this, my frustrations ran the danger of creating bitterness in me. As I built myself back up, putting myself back together one piece at a time I couldn't help but imagine what if. I would pray ask that the load be lightened and sometimes whisper in my prayers, why me.

You don't need to be a religious person to experience revelations. So I'm sure everyone has had some sort of light bulb moment. Mine was the answer to that why me question to God. It wasn't when I decided I needed to change that made sense, even a fool once they hit rock bottom will conclude to need a change. It was this answer that will be the catalyst for all my efforts for all the days of my life.

We are born to struggle our life is designed for it. So to ask why me is a question you ask from a place of self-doubt. God placed a path before me that he knew I could handle if I chose to. For years I had chosen not to, I had made excuses and played the helpless victim of circumstances. This had cost me a great deal but it didn't have to keep costing me. So the answer to my whisper why me would start to grow louder and louder. Why not you?

Was I too good to struggle or too weak? Or was it that I felt unworthy of God's attention? I had to face these questions and stop asking why. This was my reality, it wasn't going to change simply because I decided to change. If anything it only grew worse because where I had no responsibility I now had a butt load.

Change started to seem like a job and it was. The hours were long the work went without many praise and there were no days off, the upside was it would eventually pay off. The way I started to feel, the confidence I developed, it was great. I used to be unable to look most people in the eye, I fumbled over words and felt uncertain of every portion of my life. The insecurity of a broken person living as they have allowed society to shape them to live opposed to what lives in their heart is worse than death. There is no worse prison than the one a person builds for themselves out of fear of being hurt.

In the middle of a maximum security prison doing a life sentence is where I was able to find my freedom. I had been running, I had been searching high and low when all along it was I who held the key. It's like when you're in a rush to get to work and your searching for your car keys while there in your hand. There is no reason to curse yourself, simply slow down it's only as bad as we make it.

I Confess

Derrel Moore

Confessions of the accused

Chapter 17

Thank God I survived being Lil Dee

With all the guns sprayed at me with sincere efforts of men to end my young life, I can only thank God I survived. Yet I must call attention to much more subtle but equally deadly attempts on my life.

As a boy the things I was exposed to as well as my naturally curious mind shouldn't be ignored. To disturb and tamper with the psychological makeup of a child runs the risk of disturbing that child completely. With this in mind we must do better in how we love and protect our babies.

From knee high I was under attack from all angels. My brain was mush and almost immediately it was being molded to fail. Brain cells were corrupted, programmed, then I was unleashed upon the world and expected to be fully responsible for my behaviors.

The over indulgences I observed as a child showed up in how the boy I became over indulged on every level. One of my indulgences was my promiscuity, my behavior was on the level of a rock star on tour.

I had sexual relations with females whose name I didn't know and it didn't matter where we were. I would have sex in cars on the sides of houses on the ground, inside abandoned houses. It didn't matter and neither did the sex. I used it to quell the pain, the insecurity and fear. As others would chain smoke I abused my body and it put me at risk.

I was having sex with nameless females, I wasn't using any form of protection at all. There were days when I would have sex with three and four different women in the same day without the least bit of regard for safety. I didn't think about the dangers of this, I didn't care. I never once stopped to consider the consequences at all. I can't recall one day that I felt as though what I was doing was somehow wrong.

I can remember one day a young girl approached me standing on a porch on Lopere street in Buffalo New York at a friends house. She was no more than fourteen, she didn't ask my name didn't even say hi. Her words to me were do you want to have sex and she wasn't that polite in her language. I immediately said yes, took her inside the house and had sex with her. We didn't share words, it wasn't special and when it was over she left as quickly as she came.

I know now I should have been shocked by her words and I should have refused. I didn't have the ability to be shocked or feel it was wrong. I never seen her again and I don't know her story but I would bet my life hers was just as complex as my own. I think our hurt souls connected. She recognized I was like her and my troubled heart called to hers. This is how I make sense of it and try to romanticize it today. In my heart I know it was two troubled teens going unnoticed and properly nurtured. I can only pray for her and all those like her that I encountered as I wrongfully acted out my pain.

I often think of my reckless behaviors especially the sexual ones and wonder if there's children out there that I conceived that I don't know about. In my experience there's always a price to pay for reckless behavior. I was blessed not to contract in deadly disease and I know this had to be by the grace of God alone. So it often troubles me that I've yet to receive my consequence for my behaviors.

Bullets flew past my head more than once, I've seen the fire from that missile up close. To this day I still have a scar on my head as a direct result of bullets in pursuit of my end. These were warnings and I had each one as a opportunity to change my course in life. These events never caused me to think twice, if anything they would inspire me to raise the level of my gross behaviors.

I can remember a car pulling up on me as I was about to cross the street. A machine gun styled weapon, the kind only meant to be used in world wars, was pushed out the window into my stomach to cut me in half with bullets. I stood frozen, my quick thought was, "I knew it would end this way, I don't care", and then the gun's firing pen clicked. The gun hadn't been chambered with a bullet. I quickly retreated through the yard as the gunman corrected his error, soon sending a barrage of bullets in high pursuit of my sixteen year old, one hundred and fifty-five pound body. He missed and now I would respond in a way he would forever regret.

A person with any sense would have reflected on how close they had come to death. However I had no sense, I became arrogant, I believed myself to be unstoppable. So I got my own weapon of choice and the first place I went was to the gunman mother's house. I had eaten at this home even slept there, now I had gone to cause carnage. Thank God she was outside when I approached, she was a sweet precious lady. I greeted her, told her to tell her sons I came by and left without incident. The sight of her had appealed to whatever humanity was left.

This didn't last sixty seconds, I went directly to one of the gunmen's child's mother house. The baby was an infant and I had no regard for this fact. I wanted him to feel what I couldn't, fear. In truth fear is what was driving me in life but I didn't know this. At the time I thought I was fearless and I was trying to establish fear in everyone that threatened my existence. They needed to feel this because I refused to.

When we got to the house my comrade at the time, Monet, tried to point out that this guy's car wasn't there so we should keep going. He had no idea that I didn't care if he was there or not. I planned to leave my presence where he slept by way of a magazine of gunfire. I was beyond being reasoned with.

Then God intervened and the weight on my heart shifted as I seen the mother and child walk onto the porch. I got out of the cab we were in told the cab driver, who was my usual for these types of things, to drive up the street then turn back around and pick me up. Monet tried to protest again but I cut him off and he stopped trying.

The following events have always had many perceptions, here's the truth; I waited for the mother and child to enter the home. I ran on the porch knowing she had a hallway she had to walk down before unlocking another door to her downstairs apartment to enter the front room. I purposely shot into the home while she was out of the line of fire through the front window. I wasn't a reckless shooter, I had actually lessons while I lived in Bradford. I had friends who taught me, we used to play a shooting game called pitching quarters. This is a game where you pitch a quarter into a ditch in the woods and make a attempt to shoot it. I wasn't that good but I was good enough to prevent these bullets from hitting this mother and child.

However I didn't tell Monet this is what I had done. I wanted everyone, especially the man who tried to kill me to think my bullets had missed due to a miracle. I wanted everyone to see me as a madman and they did.

The irony is that I really thought I did the right thing by the female and her child. I saw what I had done as a good deed, this is how sick and how far from reality I had been. These are some of the laundry list of examples of how I lived and played with death as well as insanity. I could spend days talking about the many events that could have easily lead to my death. Instead I would rather acknowledge the presence of life as I lived so recklessly.

This presence existed in ways I didn't recognize at all nor did I know how to appreciate. I used to count myself as lucky and no way did I feel there was any purpose.

The presence of God, guiding events in a fashion that I could eventually rise above my pain was even more evident during my incarceration. I came to state prison angry, filled with frustration and ready to continue living out my pain. In many ways I actually did, but it was always controlled to a degree.

I never acted violently and hurt people as I had previously done. I involved myself with certain activities in prison that had the potential to lead to this violent behavior. I often dealt with drugs and made large sums of money in jail. This often leads to violence and new criminal charges. I would always come extremely close to getting caught by staff or seriously hurt by prisoners out of envious motivations. Both always failed to work to cause me any serious harm. As I had done before, I would believe I was special and couldn't be touched due to my genius. In truth there has always been this God presence, allowing me to take my knocks but making sure I could recover from them.

Well I have taken more knocks than I can count, I don't think our numerical system goes that high and I know I'm not done yet. However I'm no longer that boy that don't care. I no longer take chances with my life as if it has no value. I've stopped making excuses for my life and the plight of my existence. I know what was my fault as well as what wasn't. I have forgiven all my victimizers and I've forgiven myself for having lived my life as a victim.

I still find myself incarcerated and I don't know when or if I'll ever be released. I'm working on it and praying that I will achieve it because I would like to help repair the hearts as well as the minds of troubled youth. My apology, my remorse and the way I will pay my debt back to the society I helped to harm will be from my works not just my words.

Today even as I write these words from a cage there's a smile on my face and deep inside my heart. I lived a life of crime, I was reckless on every level, I've been tested in ways great people have, and I survived. I thank God that I stand tested, I stand unbroken, pushed to the limits, yet I can proudly say I survived being me.....

Confessions of the accused

Chapter 18

Free at last, thank God Almighty

On March 27, 2017 after more than a month long battle with the judicial system about what stipulations to release me under, on my daughters twenty second birthday, I was released. I had waited so long and been told no so many times that by the time it became a reality the desire to do any of the typical things one can imagine was no longer a desire.

So much had changed, I had lost my brother Shamel to gun violence, my little cousin Quan as well, my family was splintered and beyond repair. Nothing was as I had imagined, not even the things I thought I properly managed. I came home to a city full of strangers and very little transitional support.

There was a few people that did key things that allowed me to adjust and my cousin who is much more like a brother gave me a place to stay when my own plans exploded. Besides this, I was left to figure it out alone and I screwed up a bit due to my pride.

All the big dreams I had got put on hold or destroyed due to parole rules and laws that should not apply to me. I was told no, no, no to all my ideas. I was even denied permission to go back to school until I fought hard for it, then I was allowed but after passing my entry exams at Bryant and Stratton with flying colors I was discriminated against due to my criminal record as a sixteen year old.

The old me would have folded and gave in to the negativity, used it as my excuse and allowed anger to rule. Instead I decided to be patient and not get caught up in the devils lure. I would be lying if I said it's been easy or that I have not made mistakes. I made plenty and I'm not done yet but I have not resorted to that boy I was. I have outgrown him and I'm proud to say I've stayed clear of temptation.

I have been home more than a year now and I have not begged or stolen. I have not made a promise I didn't keep to myself and I'm now prepared to execute my dreams and began to create the outreach programs to change the make up of my community.

I can go on and on about all I did since home or all I plan to do, or I can simply do it. I choose to do it, but before I close let me stress this. I am here by the grace of God alone and I'm grateful. I have not been the best I can be as of yet but I'm not the boy that started this journey.

I want the people that have been of help to know I'm forever grateful and the people who have tried to stand in my way with lies and bad deeds to know I forgive them for their missteps. May God reward us all accordingly.

Confessions of the accused

Conclusion

  I made this book as short as possible and left out as much as I could. This book wasn't made to somehow praise my bad behaviors, nor to highlight my troubled childhood. Furthermore it is not meant to profit off my storied past. I did this to expose some of the complex issues in the black and brown communities in America.

  We need help and I offer just a glimpse into the mindset of our children who eventually become troubled adults with more children. This alarming reality isn't going to go away on it's own. Nor is the answer more prisons to house the results of society's failings where it concerns this issue.

  As a product of this environment I caused pain to many innocent people. If you conclude that I have no redeemable qualities, nor those like me, then consider those hurt by me and those that will be hurt by others like me. This isn't a black or brown issue alone, this is a issue that affects the world and all it's inhabitants. These issues are not isolated to the streets of Buffalo. At the age of fourteen I was crossing state lines taking my hate for self to places unprepared to deal with my madness. It is easy to come to the conclusion that if those privileged don't come affect change when it is needed then eventually the unchanged will affect you.

  I recently read a very heart wrenching book about the plight of poor children in South Asia. The story was chilling, it made me want to pledge the thirty five dollars per month to take care of one child. I'm still trying to fit it in my budget if I can get a prison program that will pay me that much per month. However as I read the many stories of the cold rape and brutalities I couldn't help but notice how similar their experiences were in South Asia are to the children in the ghettos of America.

The only difference being there is no international organization in existence trying to save us. I find it troubling that we live in the world's leading nation in humanitarian work, we come to the aide of millions of people all over the world every day and no one ever came to save me from me.

I know there are many local organizations struggling to do as much as they possibly can. I commend them all for their work and compassion. This work should not be ignored and I don't pretend it doesn't exist. I will also acknowledge that our president Obama has recently created the brother's keeper initiative. I pray it will help to address the conditions of our children.

I still find this to be a small portion of all that is needed. The criminal justice system is filled with the same children that became adults stuck in a condition that they were born to not that they created. There is still two states, New York and North Carolina prosecuting children as adults. They do not have any system in place to see how that kid came to act so violently. There is simply people trained to prosecute them and others in the prison waiting to punish them. There is no one waiting to help nurture and rehabilitate them.

I have personally been one of these subjects and I have almost twenty years in prison at the original time of writing this book. There has been not one moment of one day that even one person has ever come to figure out how and why. There was only a justice system void of justice that put labels on me I could not spell, let alone actually know how to consciously be. Then I was placed in a system where you are required to become even worse of a person or become even more of a victim. It almost guarantees you to be a career criminal or a lifetime victim.

So where do we really start? Do we simply acknowledge the error, do better with our future children and forget all those of yesterday? What happens to the hearts and minds of those we have failed, those that contributed to their failures?

To you, those of my flock, you also must began to do the work. You can't continue to hurt as you have and pretend it's all good. As you talk, walk and act in ignorance you secretly hate it but it's how you know to survive. It is time to destroy this mindset and demand your humanity. The first person you must demand it from is yourself. You must seek your liberation from your falsehoods. Your worth a billion times more than you have bartered your soul for.

I know how eloquent you spoke to your spirit and convinced yourself "they" did that to you. How "they" designed it all this way just to stick it to you. I'm not here to point fingers we have all played our roles. My prayer is that you stop focusing on what "they" did or did not do long enough to reflect on you.

They may never come, they may never help and that may never change. Whoever "they" may be to you, it is time that you be more of a friend to yourself than "they" have ever been or will be. Please do better for yourself, liberate yourself from the chains you have wrapped around you. Appeal to your own humanity and if they never try to do you any good it will not matter one bit because you will have done enough for yourself.

Moms, dads, uncles, aunts, siblings, friends, I apologize. I simply don't have all the answers, the truth is no one does. I pray you will love on your troubled children harder and fight for their liberation from the pain which inspires their madness. Do not give up on them no matter how easy they make it. As even a dirty rodent has redeemable qualities, if you give the effort surely you can find many in mankind.

I have done as best as I can with my current hand and I promise as a redeemed soul I'll continue to pay back my fellow man. Many will decide that I'm just an animal that deserves all I have gotten. You have every right to your opinion and feelings. I can only ask or suggest, if you care to judge be daring enough to save. Take your judgment to the troubled communities across our nation and appeal to the hearts of the lost with compassion and a helping hand.

Last I ask the readers to please check your current laws of your state, make sure children are not being prosecuted by our justice system. For the residence of New York and North Carolina appeal to your local government to change the age limit for those that are prosecuted as adults. The current law is that people under eighteen can be prosecuted as adults. This allows prosecutors to send boys and girls to adult prison for the rest of their lives for mistakes made at sixteen years of age.

In our society we should never conclude that a child can't change. A child whose brain has yet to develop skills should never be sentenced to the rest of their lives in prison. This speaks more to our short comings as a society than it does to the actions of a child. We must do better and the first step is to demand this law be changed.

Please Don't Put This Down And Forget The Lost Children Of Our Communities.

Made in the USA
Columbia, SC
30 July 2018